OECD *Ec*

Electronic Books

The OECD, recognising the strategic role of electronic publishing, issues the OECD ***Economic Surveys***, both for the Member countries and for countries of Central and Eastern Europe covered by the Organisation's Centre for Co-operation with Economies in Transition, as electronic books – incorporating the text, tables and figures of the printed version. The information will appear on screen in an identical format, including the use of colour in graphs.

The electronic book, which retains the quality and readability of the printed version throughout, will enable readers to take advantage of the new tools that the ACROBAT software (included with the diskette) provides by offering the following benefits:

- ❑ User-friendly and intuitive interface
- ❑ Comprehensive index for rapid text retrieval, including a table of contents, as well as a list of numbered tables and figures
- ❑ Rapid browse and search facilities
- ❑ Zoom facility for magnifying graphics or for increasing page size for easy readability
- ❑ Cut and paste capabilities
- ❑ Printing facility
- ❑ Reduced volume for easy filing/portability

Working environment: DOS, Windows or Macintosh

Subscription:	FF 1 800	US$317	£200	DM 545

Complete 1994/1995 series on CD-ROM:

	FF 2 000	US$365	£220	DM 600

Please send your order to OECD Electronic Publications or, preferably, to the Centre or bookshop with whom you placed your initial order for this Economic Survey.

Mine Orday

OECD ECONOMIC SURVEYS

1995-1996

TURKEY

ORGANISATION FOR ECONOMIC CO-OPERATION AND DEVELOPMENT

ORGANISATION FOR ECONOMIC CO-OPERATION AND DEVELOPMENT

Pursuant to Article 1 of the Convention signed in Paris on 14th December 1960, and which came into force on 30th September 1961, the Organisation for Economic Co-operation and Development (OECD) shall promote policies designed:

– to achieve the highest sustainable economic growth and employment and a rising standard of living in Member countries, while maintaining financial stability, and thus to contribute to the development of the world economy;
– to contribute to sound economic expansion in Member as well as non-member countries in the process of economic development; and
– to contribute to the expansion of world trade on a multilateral, non-discriminatory basis in accordance with international obligations.

The original Member countries of the OECD are Austria, Belgium, Canada, Denmark, France, Germany, Greece, Iceland, Ireland, Italy, Luxembourg, the Netherlands, Norway, Portugal, Spain, Sweden, Switzerland, Turkey, the United Kingdom and the United States. The following countries became Members subsequently through accession at the dates indicated hereafter: Japan (28th April 1964), Finland (28th January 1969), Australia (7th June 1971), New Zealand (29th May 1973), Mexico (18th May 1994), the Czech Republic (21st December 1995) and Hungary (7th May 1996). The Commission of the European Communities takes part in the work of the OECD (Article 13 of the OECD Convention).

Publié également en français.

Table of contents

Boxes

Tables

Text

Annexes

Statistical annex and structural indicators

Figures

Text

BASIC STATISTICS OF TURKEY

THE LAND

Area (thousand sq. km)	779	Major cities, 1990 (thousand inhabitants):	
Agricultural area (thousand sq. km)	275	Istanbul	7 309
Forests (thousand sq. km)	202	Ankara	3 237
		Izmir	2 695

THE PEOPLE

Population, 1995 (million)	60.8	Civilian labour force, 1995 (million)	21.3
Per sq. km, 1995	78	Civilian employment	19.9
Annual rate of change of population, 1995	2.0	Agriculture, forestry, fishing	9.4
		Industry	2.9
		Construction	1.1
		Services	6.5

PRODUCTION

GDP, 1995 (TL billion)	7 554 757	Origin of GDP, 1995 (per cent):	
Per head (US$)	2 717	Agriculture, forestry, fishing	15.0
Gross fixed investment, 1995 (TL billion)	1 786 276	Industry	27.0
Per cent of GDP	23.6	Construction	5.6
Per head (US$)	642	Services	52.4

THE GOVERNMENT

Public consumption, 1995 (per cent of GDP)	11.1	Public debt, end-1995 (per cent of GDP)	48.3
Central government current revenue, 1995		Domestic	18.0
(per cent of GDP)	18.6	Foreign	30.2

FOREIGN TRADE

Commodity exports, 1995, f.o.b.		Commodity imports, 1995, c.i.f.	
(per cent of GDP)	13.1	(per cent of GDP)	21.6
Main exports (per cent of total exports):		Main imports (per cent of total imports):	
Agriculture	10.7	Investment goods	29.4
Mining	1.9	Consumption goods	12.4
Industry	87.4	Inttermediate goods	50.0
		Crude oil	8.2

THE CURRENCY

Monetary unit: Turkish lira		Currency unit per US$, average of daily figures:	
		1993	10 966
		1994	29 778
		1995	45 738

Note: An international comparison of certain basic statistics is given in an annex table.

This Survey is based on the Secretariat's study prepared for the annual review of Turkey by the Economic and Development Review Committee on 8 July 1996.

•

After revisions in the light of discussions during the review, final approval of the Survey for publication was given by the Committee on 22 July 1996.

•

The previous Survey of Turkey was issued in April 1995.

Introduction

Following years of high public sector borrowing requirements (PSBRs) and inflation in excess of 50 per cent a year, a sharp deterioration in public sector and external deficits triggered a loss of confidence in the Turkish lira and a financial crisis in early 1994. An ambitious stabilisation programme was launched in April 1994 to restore sound public sector finances through sharp cuts in government expenditure and special tax measures, and in the longer-term through structural reforms. In the event, the PSBR fell from 12 to 8 per cent of GDP between 1993 and 1994, while GDP fell by 5½ per cent. Inflation remained very high, with consumer price inflation hitting a peak of 130 per cent in January 1995, as the PSBR continued to feed monetary growth.

The Turkish economy recovered strongly in 1995 and inflation fell until the summer as the authorities pursued key aspects of the April 1994 stabilisation programme. Real GDP grew 7.3 per cent (far more than expected), while the current account shifted into deficit in the last two months of the year. Latent pressures emerged after September 1995 with the calling of early elections for 24 December 1995. Inflation reaccelerated with the six monthly annualised rise in wholesale prices reaching 106 per cent in June 1996. Chapter I briefly reviews recent economic developments and assesses the economic outlook for the coming two years.

No single party emerged with a Parliamentary majority in the elections. A (minority coalition) government was formed in March 1996, but resigned in early June; a new coalition government took office in early July. This on-going policy vacuum has proved costly in terms of the stabilisation effort. Inflation finished well above its 1995 programme target. And while the PSBR to GDP ratio declined to 6½ per cent in 1995, it risks rising in 1996, owing to higher government spending and exceptionally high rates of interest being paid on Turkish government debt. In addition, income distribution probably widened further, and the structural agenda has been substantially delayed (with the notable exception of customs union with the EU). The major challenge facing the new government is to establish a credible financial strategy for achieving manageable public finances, lower inflation and sustainable economic growth in the medium term. Chapter II discusses salient features of fiscal and monetary policies as well as the banking system.

A viable medium-term stabilisation programme will require vigorous structural reform, *inter alia* rationalisation of the loss making State economic enterprises (SEEs), accelerated privatisation, a widening of the tax base and reform of the deficit-ridden social security system. Entry into EU customs union on 1 January 1996 is a unique opportunity to open up the economy to greater competition and to downsize the bloated and inefficient public sector. These issues, and the compelling need to shift potential resource savings towards raising Turkey's comparatively low basic health and education standards are discussed in Chapter III.

Turkey also faces an important challenge in the coming decades to upskill its workforce and to provide good jobs for its young, rapidly growing and urbanising population. Implementing the OECD's Jobs Strategy in a Turkish context is discussed in Chapter IV. Strong economic performance in 1995 clearly demonstrated the dynamism of the private sector and its flexibility in adapting to shocks. The key missing elements in ensuring better and stronger job creation on a sustained basis remain a more efficient and smaller public sector and more vigorous structural reform. Conclusions of the Survey are presented in Chapter V.

Following the finalisation of this report, the Refah/DYP government approved in early July several new measures. These initiatives included:

- a 50 per cent increase in civil service pay and pensions versus a 30 per cent budgeted increase (which could directly raise the PSBR by 0.8 per cent of GDP);
- a 102 per cent increase in the minimum wage;
- increases in agricultural subsidies (approved in August).

(continued on next page)

(continued)

These spending initiatives could raise the PSBR by some 1¼ per cent of GDP. But, the government subsequently announced an August "resources package" of $10 bn. including:

- 11 new revenue measures, including the accelerated privatisation of Telecom, other public asset sales, higher government fees and charges, the abolition of the compulsory savings scheme (effectively lowering the government wage bill) and extension of the Resource Utilisation Fund levy to foreign financed imports;
- encouraging the repatriation of foreign exchange deposits held by Turkish correspondent banks;
- the issuing of foreign exchange denominated Treasury bills;
- centralisation of government cash management practices in order to lower borrowing costs;
- enhanced conditions for attracting remittances from expatriate workers.

The government hopes to realise a third of the extra revenue (1¼ per cent of GDP) in 1996, which would in principle be consistent with the original PSBR forecast of 7.5 per cent of GDP. However, the actual outcome is likely to be worse owing to spending overruns, notably on debt service.

I. Recent economic developments and prospects

Overview

The growth of total domestic demand surged to some 12 per cent in 1995, far higher than expected a year earlier. Despite a widening in the trade deficit, real GDP growth in 1995 was a robust 7.3 per cent, some 2½ percentage points above the estimated growth of potential output. By the third quarter of 1995, the level of output had re-attained its pre-recession level (Figure 1), though a modest output gap may still persist. Labour market data (available to October 1995) indicate a continuing high, albeit falling level of excess labour supply. High inflation remains a problem. Wholesale price (WPI) inflation in the 12 months to December 1995 was 65 per cent, compared with its programme target of 40 per cent; and since September 1995 six-monthly WPI inflation has picked up sharply. The visible trade deficit also widened significantly during 1995, as imports (notably of investment goods) surged. However, the current account deficit remained small until October owing to strong growth in invisibles earnings. Foreign reserves were built up rapidly to record levels by October 1995, reflecting large scale short-term capital inflows. However, reserves were substantially run down prior to the December 1995 elections, and have been only partially rebuilt to date in the face of continuing political uncertainty.

Demand and output

Output growth rebounded sharply in 1995, following a large drop in 1994. Compared with its year-earlier level, output began to grow vigorously from the second quarter. Agricultural output was up 2.6 per cent for 1995 as a whole, but construction fell by 4.7 per cent. Industry and retail trade staged strong double digit recoveries (Table 1). Data for the first three months of 1996 suggest

Figure 1. **KEY ASPECTS OF ECONOMIC ACTIVITY**

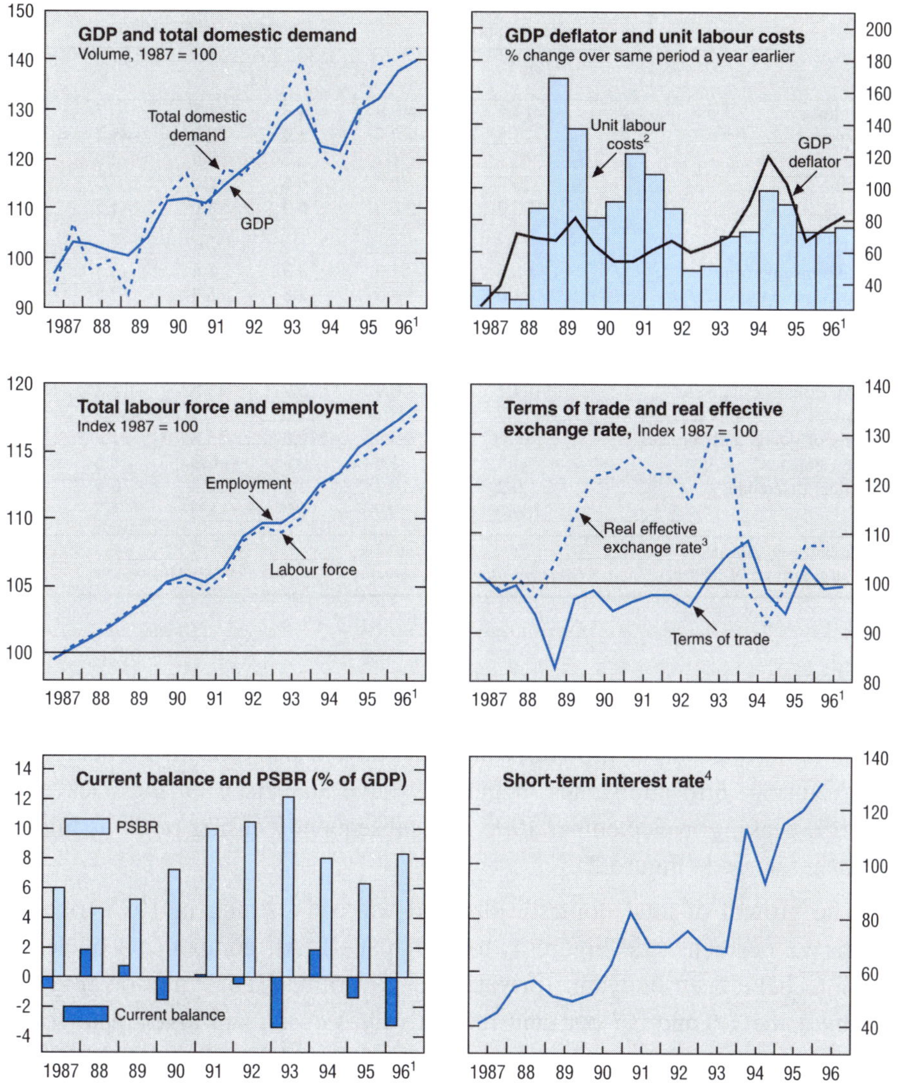

1. OECD estimates for 1996.
2. Total economy.
3. Calculated using consumer price inflation relative to Turkey's trading partners.
4. Three-month treasury bill.

Source: OECD, *National Accounts, Main Economic indicators,* and estimates.

Table 1. **Supply and use of resources**

	1990 Share of GDP in current prices	1991	1992	1993	1994	1995
		Percentage volume changes				
Supply						
Agriculture	17.5	–0.9	4.3	–1.3	–0.7	2.6
Industry	25.5	2.7	5.9	8.2	–5.7	12.1
Construction	6.3	1.1	6.2	7.9	–2.0	–4.7
Services	50.7	0.6	6.6	11.0	–7.2	7.9
GDP	100.0	0.9	6.0	8.0	–5.5	7.3
Demand						
Private consumption	68.6	1.9	3.3	8.4	–5.3	7.6
Public consumption	11.0	4.5	3.8	5.4	–3.5	6.7
Investment	22.9	1.2	4.3	24.9	–15.9	8.3
Final domestic demand	102.4	1.9	3.6	12.4	–8.2	7.7
Stockbuilding[1]	1.7	–2.9	1.6	1.2	–4.6	4.7
Total domestic demand	104.1	–0.9	5.2	13.5	–12.3	12.7
Exports of goods and services	13.3	3.1	11.0	7.7	15.2	6.7
Imports of goods and services	17.6	–5.3	10.9	35.8	–21.9	30.0
Foreign balance[1]	–4.3	1.8	–0.3	–6.2	8.6	–5.1
Statistical discrepancy[1]	0.2	0.1	1.0	0.5	–0.9	–0.1
GDP	100.0	0.9	6.0	8.0	–5.5	7.3

1. Contribution to growth.
Source: State Institute of Statistics, *Turkish Economy, Statistics and Analysis,* and State Planning Organisation.

continuing strong output growth, with GDP up 8.2 per cent on its year earlier level. Capacity utilisation rates in industry have also risen on the back of the recovery, peaking in September 1995 and subsequently easing back, as business investment surged (Figure 2).

The growth of total domestic demand was very strong in 1995, rising by perhaps 12 per cent (see Figure 1, top left panel). All components of demand appear to have been buoyant:[1] private and government consumption may have risen by some 7.6 and 6.7 per cent respectively. Gross fixed investment rose by 8.3 per cent, as business investment expanded by 14.9 per cent (while public investment was cut by 16.9 per cent). Strong private sector spending may also have been affected by the resumption of credit growth, as bank lending resumed following the 1994 credit crunch.[2]

Such a strong recovery in domestic demand and output was unexpected; and it is unclear what sources of income underpinned the 8.7 per cent rise in real

Figure 2. **INDUSTRIAL TRENDS**
Seasonally adjusted

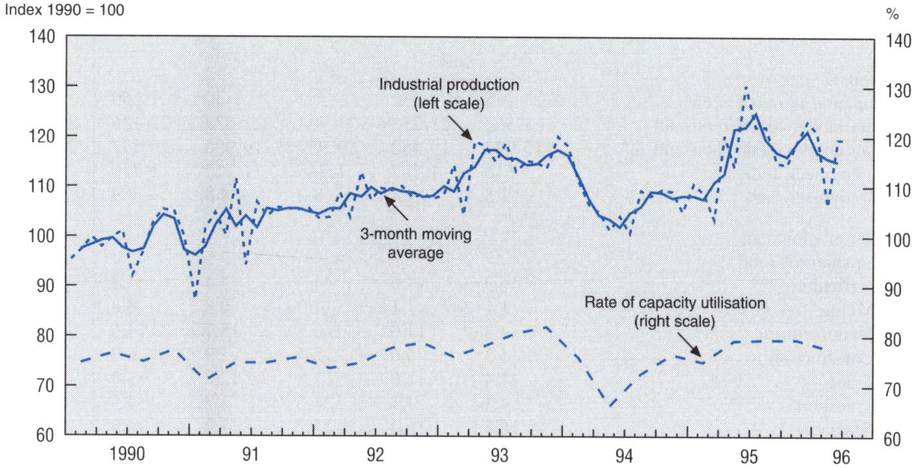

Source: OECD, *Main Economic Indicators.*

private disposable income. In particular, the sharp drop in private and public sector real wages (of some 20 per cent in 1994[3]) appears to have been only partially restored in 1995. On the other hand, agricultural incomes rose somewhat in real terms. Profits of large firms were probably quite strong in 1995, owing to strong activity, and there was a large further rise in real interest income on government bonds.[4] Nonetheless, there is considerable uncertainty concerning the level and composition of national income,[5] with some estimates suggesting under-reporting of up to a third.[6]

Labour market trends

Labour market analysis is constrained by the availability of timely data. Preliminary results of the October 1995 semi-annual Household Labour Force Survey indicate that the unemployment rate was 6.6 per cent, down from 7.9 per cent a year earlier (Table 2). Under-employment was estimated at some 6.3 per cent and urban unemployment remained high.

Table 2. **Labour market indicators**

	1990	1991	1992	1993	1994	1995
	October					April
Population 12 and over						
Participation ratio, per cent	55	52	52	50	50	50
Civilian labour force, thousand	21 562	21 238	21 703	21 628	22 136	22 446
Civilian employment, thousand	19 947	19 452	19 959	19 906	20 397	20 833
Unemployment, thousand	1 616	1 787	1 745	1 722	1 740	1 613
Unemployment rate	7.5	8.4	8.0	8.0	7.9	7.2
Civilian employment						
As a share of total						
Agriculture	46.9	47.6	44.7	43.4	44.2	47.4
Mining	1.1	1.1	1.0	0.8	0.8	0.8
Manufacturing	14.8	14.0	16.5	15.1	14.6	14.1
Construction	5.2	5.6	5.4	5.9	6.0	5.5
Trade	11.4	11.6	12.5	12.8	13.0	12.3
Transport	4.3	4.1	4.2	4.8	4.5	4.0
Other	16.3	16.0	15.7	17.2	16.9	15.9
Population 15-64						
Participation ratio, per cent	60.3	58.0	57.3	56.7	56.1	56.5
Civilian labour force, thousand	20 033	19 728	20 294	20 496	20 758	20 980
Civilian employment, thousand	18 520	18 049	18 629	18 828	19 085	19 421
Unemployment, thousand	1 513	1 678	1 665	1 669	1 673	1 560
Unemployment rate	7.6	8.5	8.2	8.1	8.1	7.4

Source: State Institute of Statistics, *Haber Bülteni: April 1995 Labour Force Survey* and *Household Labour Force Surveys.*

The main problems facing the labour market are structural. These issues are discussed in greater depth in Chapter IV. In particular – given the rapid growth of the working-age population, the low average age of the population and rapid urbanisation – rapid job creation is needed merely to hold the unemployment rate steady. Particular problem areas are upskilling of the labour force, high urban unemployment and improving the transition from school to work through improved vocational training.

Costs and prices

Inflation in 1995 again proved much stronger than programmed. Following stronger than expected inflation in the last months of 1994, the government raised its projections for WPI inflation over the 12 months to December 1995, from 22.5 per cent to just under 40 per cent – and made its fiscal plans on this basis. Following a modest easing from May through August (in part seasonal), monthly rates of inflation picked up in the wake of strong liquidity growth (see Chapter II). In the event, the WPI rose 65 per cent in the 12 months ending December, while the rise in the CPI was even more pronounced (Figure 3). Inflation continued at a brisk pace through June 1996 (the latest month available), with 12-month rates of increase in the wholesale and consumer prices at 76.2 per cent and 82.9, respectively; on a six monthly (annualised) basis comparable rates were even higher at some 106 and 87 per cent, respectively, partially reflecting seasonal factors.[7]

Domestic cost pressure appears to have played a secondary, albeit significant, role in high inflation. Wage data cover only a small fraction of the labour force, but imply that real wages of dependent employees rose only modestly in 1995, following large losses in 1994. However, real agricultural incomes may have increased somewhat more,[8] and business profits and interest incomes were also quite strong. These trends imply a continuation of the large shift in factor income distribution away from wage earners, typically to higher income households with higher savings propensities.[9]

The OECD Secretariat's analysis suggests that the fundamental reason for continuing high inflation is the excessive level of the PSBR and its monetisation. In 1995, preliminary estimates suggest that a large proportion of the PSBR continued to be monetised (roughly 12 per cent of the change in nominal 1995 central government spending was directly financed through central bank advances). Indeed had the Central Bank not undertaken substantial open market operations, inflation could well have been even higher in 1995 (see Chapter II).

Disappointing inflation performance during 1995 and early 1996 may be largely traced to excessive growth of the money supply in the first six months of 1995, and rapid growth of credit to the government since September 1995 (Figure 4). During this first period, foreign reserves recovered sharply reflecting currency substitution back into Turkish lira. In the event, the resulting increase in domestic liquidity was not sufficiently sterilised. And, while monetary growth slowed in the third quarter of 1995, its effects were largely offset by a weaker "real" exchange rate after September. In sum, poor inflation outcomes since early 1995 can largely be explained by strong growth in the monetary aggregates,

Figure 3. **INFLATION DEVELOPMENTS**

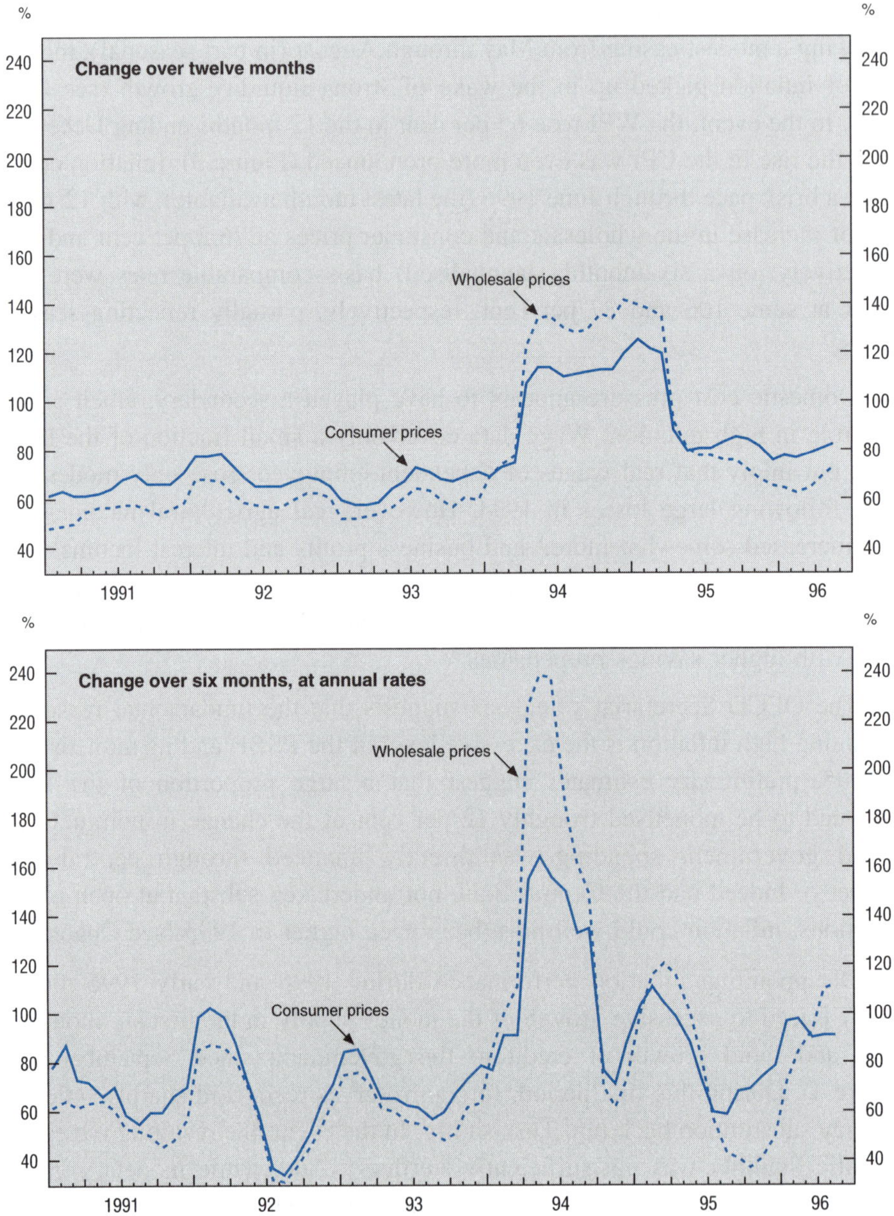

Source: OECD, *Main Economic Indicators.*

Figure 4. **MONEY SUPPLY**

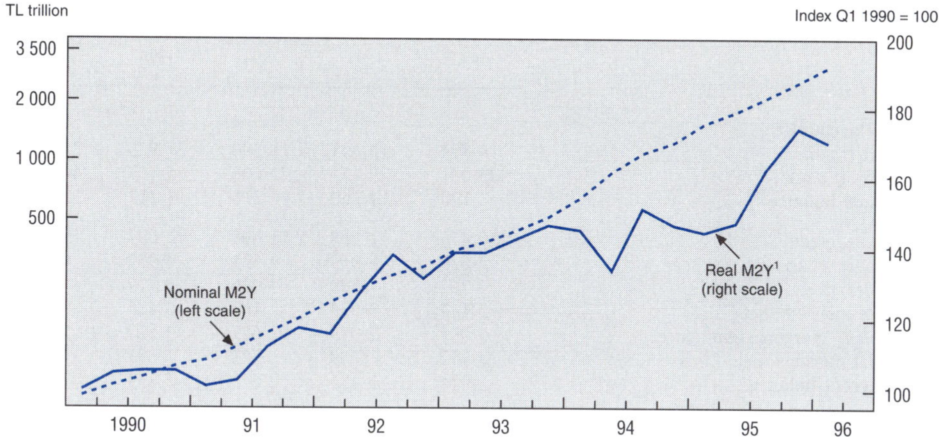

1. M2Y deflated by the wholesale price index. M2Y equals M2 plus domestic foreign exchange deposits. M2 is the sum of currency in circulation, sight deposits with deposit money banks and deposits with the Central Bank.

Source: Central Bank of Turkey, *Monthly Statistical Bulletin*, and State Institute of Statistics, *Monthly Bulletin*.

even in the short run (see Annex I). Other effects, such as stronger cost pressure and rising capacity utilisation may also have contributed, but may have been masked by rapid growth of money and domestic liquidity.

External developments

Following the 1994 exchange rate crisis, Turkey's external trade and payments position has continued to attract close public scrutiny. Preliminary data indicate a current account deficit of $2.3 billion (some 1½ per cent of GDP) for 1995, after a $2.6 billion surplus in 1994 (Table 3). On present trends, a deficit of some 2 to 3 per cent of GDP would appear to pose few financing problems, especially in view of strong potential portfolio and direct investment in the wake of customs union with the EU, high foreign reserves (representing 4 months of merchandise imports) and improved access to international capital markets.

Table 3. **Balance of payments**

$ million

	1992	1993	1994	1995	1996 Programme [1]
Current account					
Export (f.o.b.)	14 891	15 611	18 390	21 975	25 400
Imports (f.o.b.)	23 081	29 771	22 606	35 187	40 500
Trade balance	–8 190	–14 160	–4 216	–13 212	–15 100
Services, credit	10 419	11 788	11 691	16 094	18 300
of which: Tourism	3 639	3 959	4 321	4 957	6 100
Services, debit	7 262	7 829	7 936	9 717	11 150
Private transfers, net	3 147	3 035	2 709	3 425	3 380
of which: Workers' remittances	3 008	2 919	2 627	3 327	3 300
Official transfers, net	912	733	383	1 071	770
Current balance	–974	–6 433	2 631	–2 339	–3 800
Capital account					
Long-term capital	2 252	5 909	933	2 417	4 680
Direct investment	779	622	559	772	1 200
Portfolio investment	2 411	3 917	1 158	1 724	3 180
Other	–938	1 370	–784	–79	300
Short-term capital	1 396	3 054	–5 127	2 305	1 620
Errors and omissions	–1 190	–2 222	1 769	2 275	0
Overall balance	1 484	308	206	4 658	2 500

1. State Planning Organisation estimates.
Source: Central Bank of Turkey, *Quarterly Bulletin,* and State Planning Organisation.

Exports of goods and services rose some 6.7 per cent in volume in 1995 as Turkey continued to gain export market share (Figure 5, panel C). However, this good performance was more than offset by a 30 per cent jump in imports of goods and services, following the previous year's slump.[10] The export/import coverage ratio dropped to some 60.6 per cent in 1995, close to its average over the previous 4 years and the visible trade deficit widened significantly (Figure 5, panel B). However, the surplus on invisibles earnings also increased in 1995, partially offsetting the widening in the trade deficit. Tourism revenue grew rapidly, as did other earnings[11] and official unrequited transfers (*cf.* Table 3). (Trade data for 1996 are not yet available, owing to changes in statistical reporting methods following Turkey's entry into customs union with the EU on 1st January 1996.)

Figure 5. **FOREIGN TRADE DEVELOPMENTS**

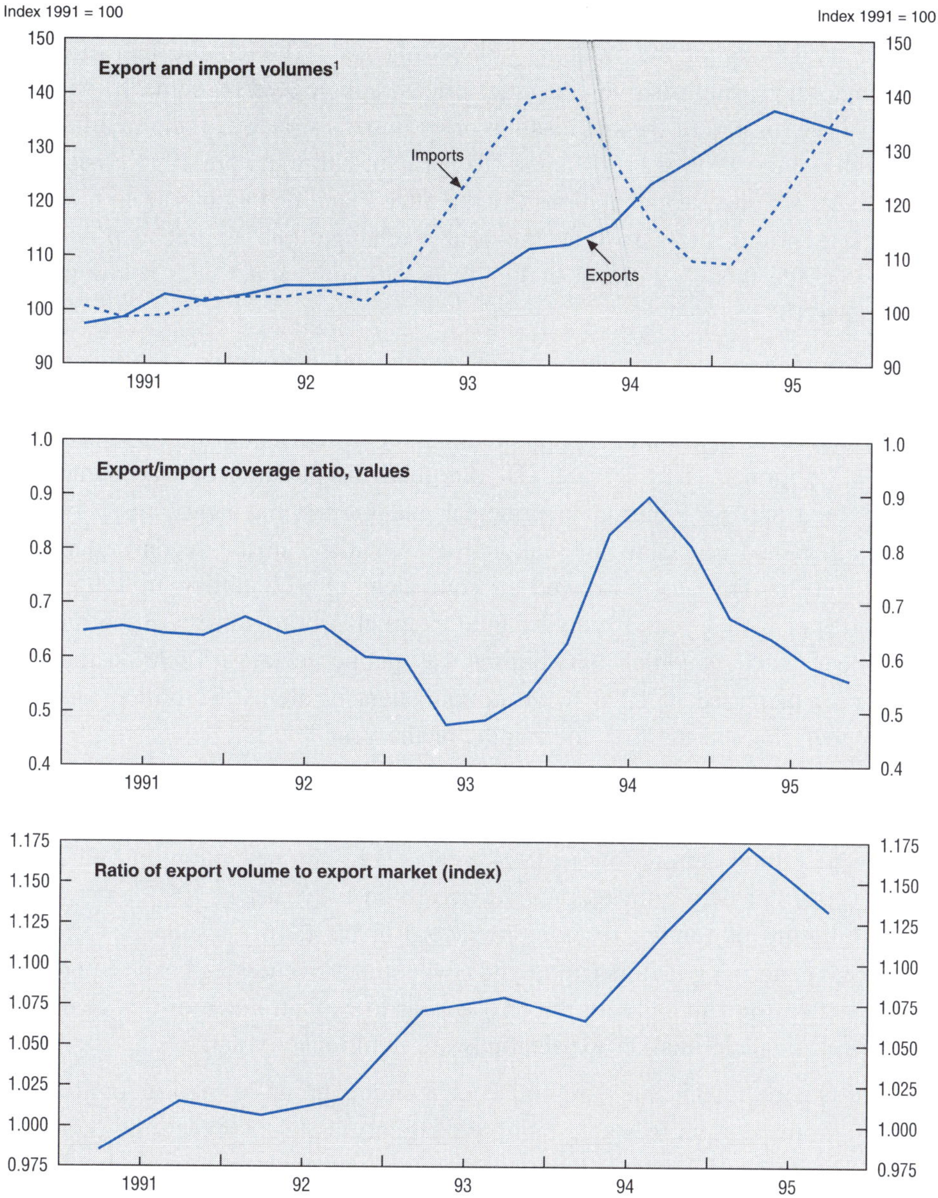

1. Using four-quarter moving average of quantity indices.

Source: State Institute of Statistics, *Summary of Monthly Trade*, and OECD.

To a large extent, the wider 1995 trade deficit reflected strong growth of domestic demand and a rebound in imports from 1994's depressed levels, rather than a weakening of international competitiveness. Though the real effective exchange rate (using relative consumer prices) appreciated by some 10 per cent during 1995 (as part of the stabilisation programme's strategy to rein in inflation), its level in June 1996 was still some 20 per cent below its pre-1994 crisis level (Figure 6). Alternative calculations (by the State Planning Organisation) based on wholesale prices indicate that the real exchange rate appreciated slightly more in 1995, though its level in June was still some 8 per cent below that of December 1993.

Financing of the current account deficit and repayment of official debt obligations posed few difficulties for most of 1995 (Figure 7). In 1995 Turkey repaid almost $10 billion to foreign creditors, of which $5.7 billion was principal and $4.3 billion in debt service. (Of this total the public sector accounted for $2.7 billion and $2.3 billion in principal and interest payments, respectively.) Turkey regained access to international debt markets in the second quarter of 1995, and the Treasury borrowed an equivalent of $2.3 billion in 1995 (with maturities of 2 to 3 years) bringing total external debt to some $73.3 billion by December 1995, of which $50 billion was public sector[12] (Table 4). Foreign borrowing increased in 1996, with an equivalent of almost $2 billion raised at longer maturities in the first six months of the year.[13]

A noteworthy feature of 1995 was the sea change in financial market sentiment towards TL denominated assets, as short-term capital flows switched from a $5 billion net outflow in 1994 to a $2.3 billion net inflow in 1995. This big reversal not only allowed debt service to be fully met in 1995,[14] but also a rapid build-up of foreign reserves to record levels ($16.7 billion in October). Although underlying factors (improved cost competitiveness and export performance, and customs union with the EU) appear to explain much of this change in sentiment, financial market expectations are notoriously volatile.

In October 1995, Standard and Poor's ratings group revised its outlook for Turkey from positive to stable citing uncertainty as to the course of economic policy. Its rating of Turkey's long-term foreign currency debt remained at B+. In May 1996, the Japan Credit Rating Agency announced that it had placed its BB+ rating of Turkey's long-term foreign currency debt under credit monitor, owing to concern about the sustainability of the incumbent coalition government.

Figure 6. **EXCHANGE RATE DEVELOPMENTS**

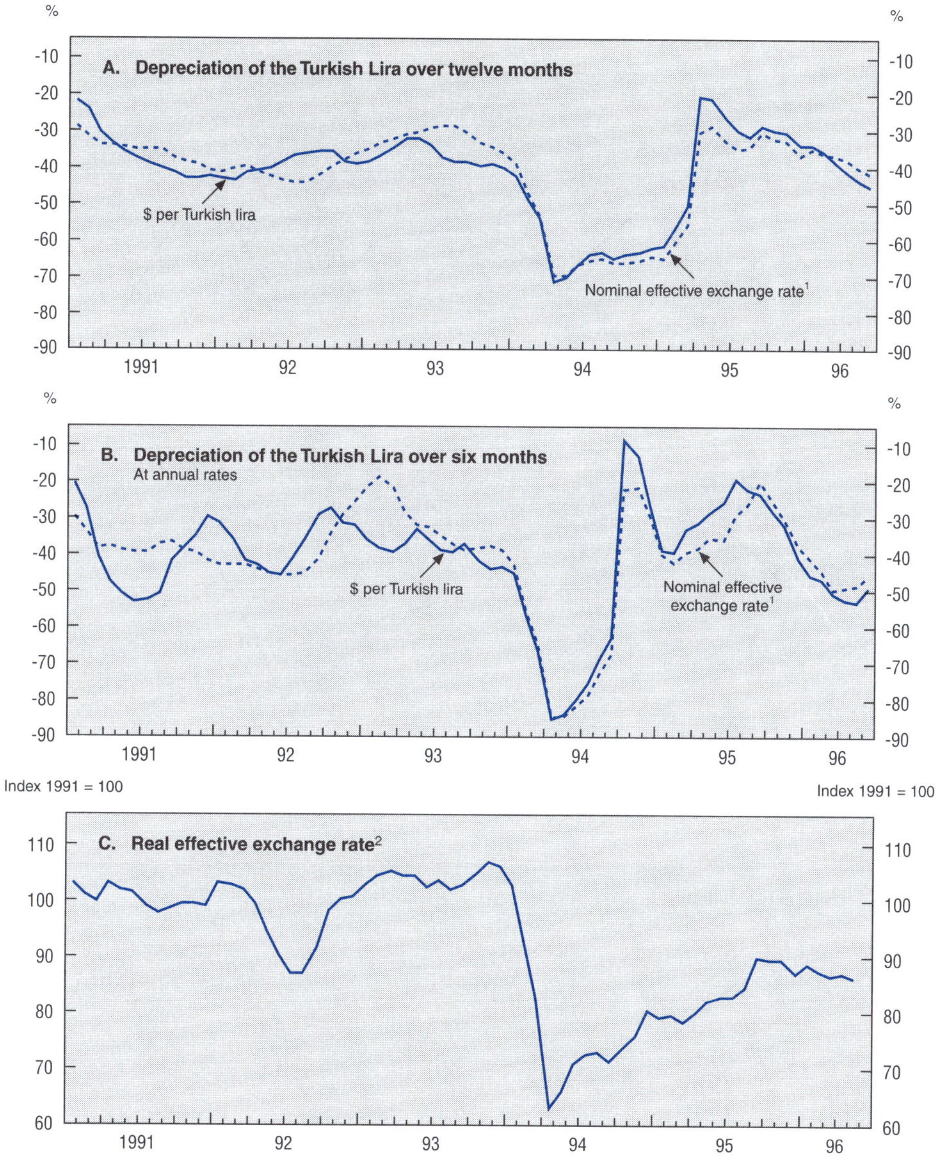

1. Trade-weighted index.
2. Calculated using consumer price inflation relative to Turkey's trading partners.
Source: OECD.

Figure 7. **CURRENT ACCOUNT AND EXTERNAL DEBT**

% of GDP

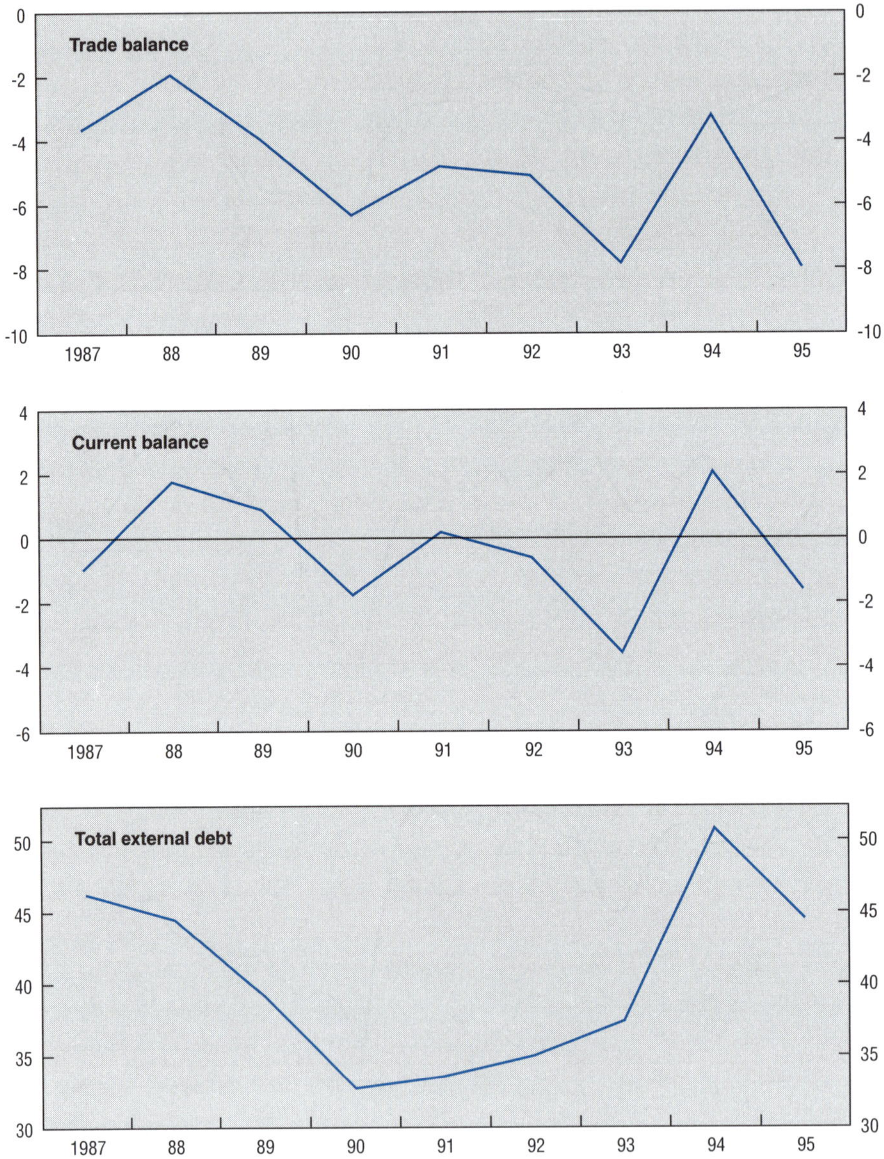

Source: Central Bank of Turkey and OECD.

Table 4. **External debt of Turkey**

Disbursed debt – end of period
$ million

	1990	1991	1992	1993	1994	1995
Medium- and long-term debt	39 535	41 372	42 932	48 823	54 291	57 577
Multilateral creditors	9 564	10 069	9 160	8 674	9 183	9 081
Bilateral creditors	12 984	14 587	15 035	18 153	20 678	21 558
Commercial banks	10 720	10 992	12 956	15 706	16 113	16 532
Private lenders	6 267	5 724	5 781	6 290	8 317	10 406
Short-term debt	9 500	9 117	12 660	18 533	11 310	15 701
Credits	5 524	6 134	10 065	15 436	8 044	11 230
Deposits	3 976	2 983	2 595	3 097	3 266	4 471
Total debt	49 035	50 489	55 592	67 356	65 601	73 278
Memorandum items (per cent):						
Total debt/GDP	32.5	33.4	34.9	37.3	50.5	44.4
Medium- and long-term debt/GDP	26.2	27.4	26.9	27.0	41.8	34.9
Short-term debt/GDP	6.3	6.0	7.9	10.3	8.7	9.5
Short-term/total debt	19.4	18.1	22.8	27.5	17.2	21.4
Total debt/foreign exchange revenue [1]	193.6	195.2	195.1	221.3	200.1	176.6
Medium- and long-term debt by borrower as per cent of total debt						
General government	52.3	54.3	51.2	45.7	51.9	47.3
SEEs	9.8	10.3	9.2	8.1	8.4	6.6
Central bank	14.9	12.9	11.1	9.8	13.1	14.3
Private sector	3.7	4.5	5.7	8.9	9.4	10.4
Debt service/GDP	4.8	5.0	5.3	4.6	7.7	6.0
Debt service/foreign exchange revenue [1]	28.6	29.0	29.2	26.2	28.6	24.0
Average maturity (year)	15.1	14.6	14.0	12.5	12.5	..

1. Foreign exchange revenue is the sum of exports, other goods and services, unrequited transfers (private).
Source: Central Bank of Turkey, *Quarterly Bulletin.*

Short-term economic prospects

The economic outlook over the coming two years is sketched out below on the following technical assumptions:

– The PSBR in 1996 is assumed to be some $8\frac{1}{2}$ per cent of GDP (1 point higher than the budget's target for a PSBR of $7\frac{1}{2}$ per cent of GDP); slower economic growth and lower inflation are assumed to pave the way for lower interest rates and a small reduction in the PSBR to some 7 to 8 per cent of GDP in 1997;

- monetary conditions are assumed to be sufficiently tight to rein in the growth of the money supply and to hold WPI inflation in 1996 to some 80 per cent and to reduce it in 1997;
- the real exchange rate remains unchanged from its level prevailing on 30 June 1996;
- oil prices average $16.60 and $15.80 a barrel in 1996 and 1997 respectively;
- growth of Turkish export markets is in the 7 to 8 per cent range in the coming two years.

Domestic interest rate developments will have a major impact on the PSBR. Interest rates have dropped substantially from their January 1996 peaks, though they remain very high, at annual rates of some 127 per cent in early July 1996. Decisive fiscal and structural action could pave the way for an eventual drop in risk premia on government debt, thereby stabilising or reducing the domestic debt service burden in 1997 and beyond.

The OECD projects that GDP growth will gradually slow to some 6 per cent in 1996. This, and continuing labour market slack, could permit a gradual, albeit slow decline in inflation to an average of some 80 per cent in 1996. The current account deficit is projected to rise to around 3½ per cent of GDP in 1997. On-going structural reform, notably of the state economic enterprises (SEEs) and the social security system, is assumed to contribute to a gradual improvement in the primary budget surplus, and lower inflation and nominal interest rates. Against this background, GDP growth could continue at some 5 per cent in 1997, with inflation falling modestly to 65 per cent and the PSBR being slowly reduced to more sustainable levels (Table 5).

The risks and uncertainties surrounding these projections are evidently quite large. External financing constraints are not a near term problem. However, the past few years have seen large scale currency substitution, and the very short maturity of domestic debt has increased the volatility of financial markets in the absence of strong and decisive policy action. The Turkish economy would appear, once again, to be at a cross-roads. Failure to establish a credible medium-term economic strategy and to restore fiscal stability could trigger a deterioration

Table 5. **Projections for 1996 and 1997**

Percentage changes, volume (1987 prices)

	1994		1995	Projections	
	Current prices TL trillion	Per cent of GDP		1996	1997
Private consumption	2 565.5	66.3	7.6	6.3	5.5
Public consumption	451.0	11.7	6.7	3.0	3.0
Gross fixed investment	946.2	24.5	8.3	9.0	7.5
Final domestic demand	3 962.7	102.4	7.7	6.8	5.9
Stockbuilding [1]	–121.4	–3.1	4.7	0.5	0.0
Total domestic demand	3 841.2	99.3	12.7	7.2	5.8
Exports of goods and services	826.4	21.4	6.7	10.0	10.0
Imports of goods and services	788.5	20.4	30.0	14.0	12.0
Statistical discrepancy [1]	–10.7	–0.3	–0.1	0.0	0.0
GDP at market prices	3 868.4	100.0	7.3	6.0	5.0
GDP implicit price deflator			81.9	80.0	65.0
Memorandum items:					
Consumer prices			93.6	80.0	65.0
Unemployment rate			7.5	7.0	6.8
Current balance ($ billion)			–2.3	–4.5	–6.0
Current balance (% of GDP)			–1.4	–2.7	–3.5

1. Change as a percentage of GDP in previous period.
Source: OECD.

in confidence and create economic instability. By the same token, sharper declines in the PSBR, inflation and debt service costs are also possible. (This potential is quite large, as the average maturity of domestic debt carrying market related interest rates is only slightly more than 4 months). But this would require a degree of social cohesion and political resolve to pursue fiscal consolidation and structural reform which has been absent over the past decade.

II. Macroeconomic policies

Even though the stabilisation policies pursued since April 1994 have halved the public sector borrowing requirement (PSBR) in relation to GDP, inflation remains stubbornly high. This indicates the strength and persistence of inflation inertia which complicates macroeconomic management by reducing the potency of monetary policy and by raising the primary budget surplus necessary to ensure continuing fiscal consolidation. This chapter first discusses fiscal and debt management policies since early 1995. These developments are analysed against the backdrop of a Medium-term Financial Strategy (MTFS) illustrating the necessary conditions to achieve sound public finances, lower inflation and stable economic growth. Monetary and exchange rate developments are analysed in the next section. A final section reviews the banking and financial system from a perspective of prudential supervision and systemic risk.

Fiscal policy

Large fiscal deficits have been at the root of macroeconomic instability in Turkey over the past decade. The PSBR has exceeded 5 per cent of GDP in every year since 1989, rising to over 10 per cent of GDP between 1991 and 1993 (Table 6). The pernicious impact of large budget deficits has been exacerbated by heavy monetary financing. Central Bank financing of the PSBR was 2¾ per cent of GDP in 1993, compared with a monetary base of around 4 per cent of GDP (provoking high inflation to restore desired "real balances", see below). The April 1994 stabilisation programme stressed the need to restore sound public finances, and measures were introduced then to lower the PSBR in 1994 and 1995. The current level of the PSBR, at 6½ per cent of GDP, nonetheless remains problematic, as structural measures to ensure sustainable medium-term public finances have been slow to be put in place.

Table 6. **Public sector finances**

	1991	1992	1993	1994	1995	1996 Programme
Budget balances (TL trillion)						
Public sector	–64.5	–116.6	–244.6	–314.3	–495.0	–1 017.1
Consolidated budget	–33.5	–47.4	–133.9	–152.2	–319.5	–861.0
Budget balances (% of GDP)						
Public sector	–10.2	–10.7	–12.3	–8.1	–6.6	–7.6
Consolidated budget	–5.3	–4.3	–6.8	–3.9	–4.2	–6.4
State economic enterprises	–3.5	–4.0	–3.2	–2.1	–0.4	–0.6
Local administrations	–0.3	–0.8	–1.0	–0.6	–0.5	–0.5
Social security institutions	–0.1	–0.2	–0.6	–0.6	–0.7	–0.3
Extra-budgetary funds	–0.9	–1.3	–0.9	–0.9	–0.7	0.2
Financing of PSBR (% of GDP)						
Central Bank	1.7	1.6	2.7	1.3	1.3	1.3
Foreign borrowing, net	0.4	1.6	1.0	–1.6	–0.9	–0.6
Domestic borrowing, net	8.1	7.5	8.6	8.4	6.2	6.9
Public sector debt stocks (% of GDP)						
Bonds and Treasury bills	8	12	13	14	15	..
Other Turkish lira debt[1]	7	6	5	7	3	..
Foreign currency debt	26	25	24	37	30	..
Total public sector debt	41	43	42	58	48	..

1. Central Bank advances and consolidated debt.
Source: State Planning Organisation.

A major constraint on Turkey's budget position is its low tax collecting capacity. In 1995, consolidated budget revenues amounted to only 18 per cent of GDP (compared with general government receipts of over 35 per cent in other OECD countries[15]). Furthermore, a substantial part of the informal economy effectively avoids tax (notably direct and social security tax), with the result that effective tax rates on the formal economy are comparatively high. Tax collection difficulties are also exacerbated by high inflation[16] and ineffective tax administration.

Significant reductions in the consolidated budget deficit were achieved between 1993 and 1995 (from 6¾ to 4 per cent of GDP), and the PSBR fell in parallel (from 12¼ to 6½ per cent of GDP).[17] In 1995, the ratio of consolidated budget revenues to GDP was little changed from 1993. Hence, all of the decline in the consolidated budget achieved during this period reflected cuts in spending as a proportion of GDP. As interest payments have risen in relation to GDP, this has necessitated sharp cuts in other spending items, notably on personnel and public investment. This strategy has delivered big short-term improvements in the PSBR, but a sustained improvement will require a wider tax base and higher tax revenue, as well as lower debt service payments.

Total debt-service payments rose from 5.9 to 7.6 per cent of GDP between 1993 and 1995, accounting for 34 per cent of total budgetary spending in 1995. This rise reflected greater reliance on domestic debt financing of the PSBR. Since the 1994 devaluation, interest rates on TL denominated debt have been very high, incorporating a large risk premium, as investors have been reluctant to hold medium or long-term debt.

The deficit due to ''off-budget'' items in the PSBR fell from 5½ to 2¼ per cent of GDP between 1993 and 1995. Most of this improvement was due to the reduced borrowing needs of state economic enterprises (SEEs). The April 1994 stabilisation programme introduced large public sector price increases to restore the financial health of the SEEs; and realistic pricing policies and harder budget constraints have since been generally maintained (despite some slippage in the period preceding the December 1995 elections). Off-budget borrowing of the social security institutions remained at some 0.7 per cent of GDP in 1995. However, the current system is a large drain in the Treasury and in need of urgent reform (see Chapter III).

Despite greater reliance on debt financing of the PSBR, total public sector debt declined from 58 per cent of GDP at the end of 1994 to 48 per cent of GDP at the end of 1995 (Table 6). Approximately two-thirds of the total public sector debt is in foreign currency. The ratio of foreign currency debt to GDP rose sharply in 1994, reflecting the large real devaluation, but fell substantially in 1995, as a result of real currency appreciation and net foreign debt repayment.[18] A primary public sector surplus of 1 per cent of GDP, money financing of the PSBR of around 1¼ per cent of GDP, and continuing high inflation helped to reduce the ratio of domestic debt to GDP from 21 to 18 per cent of GDP between 1994 and 1995.

The 1996 budget

The 1996 budget was initially presented to Parliament just prior to the decision to call an early general election in December 1995. Once the election was called, debate on the budget was suspended, although Parliament passed a provisional budget authorising spending for the first four months of 1996. The budget for the whole year was approved by Parliament in April 1996. This targets a consolidated budget deficit of TL 861 trillion, around 6½ per cent of GDP[19] (Table 7). Revenue is expected to rise significantly as a proportion of GDP, as a result of buoyant economic activity in 1995 and improved tax collection rates. Privatisation revenue is projected to rise to almost 1 per cent of GDP (almost three times higher than in 1995), although only a quarter of this is included in budget revenue. The abolition of the Mass Housing Fund and other levies previously charged on imports represented a loss of revenue, equivalent to some 1.2 per cent of GDP in 1995, but around half of this loss has been offset by increased taxation of petroleum products, alcohol, tobacco, automobiles and some luxury items.[20]

Budget spending is projected to rise from 22½ per cent of GDP in 1995 to 26 per cent in 1996. Just under a half of this increase is due to higher non-interest spending, notably on personnel, investment and transfers to the social security

Table 7. **1995 and 1996 budgets**

TL trillion

	1995 Budget	1995 Outcome	1996 Budget
Consolidated budget			
Revenues	1 133	1 377	2 650
Non-interest spending	943	1 121	2 215
Primary balance	190	257	435
Interest payments	388	576	1 296
Budget balance	–198	–319	–861
Total public sector			
Non-consolidated budget balance	–106	–176	–156
Total public sector budget balance	–304	–495	–1 017
Memorandum items:			
Consolidated budget primary balance (% of GDP)	3.2	3.3	3.7
Public sector primary balance (% of GDP)	1.5	0.9	2.5
Consolidated budget balance (% of GDP)	–3.3	–4.2	–6.5
Public sector balance (% of GDP)	–5.0	–6.6	–7.6

Source: State Planning Organisation, and OECD estimates.

institutions. Debt interest payments will rise sharply, from 7½ to 10 per cent of GDP. However, these figures exaggerate the underlying rise, since the lengthening of debt maturities from March to September 1995 effectively transferred a part of debt service from 1995 into 1996.

The primary public sector balance is projected to be in a surplus of TL 279 trillion (2 per cent of GDP) in 1996. "Off-budget" components of public sector borrowing are projected to fall as a share of GDP compared with 1995. Although the financial deficit of the social security institutions is expected to increase by a further ¼ per cent of GDP, this will be more than offset by higher transfers from the consolidated budget (Table 8).

If these budget plans are realised, the PSBR could be some 7½ per cent of GDP in 1996. This would help to lower debt as a proportion of GDP and stabilise the ratio of debt interest to GDP in 1997, as well as reducing it in later years (see Annex II). The 1996 budget targets are much more realistic than previous budgets. But the task of meeting them is challenging. Between January and May 1996, the consolidated budget deficit amounted to TL 378 trillion, while the cash deficit came to TL 429 trillion, although a primary surplus of TL 198 trillion was also realised. Nonetheless, the projected increase in revenue as a proportion of GDP is ambitious, and will require substantial effort. If this is not achieved, programmed spending plans, as well as higher-than-budgeted increases in public sector pay and pensions could raise public sector borrowing, at a time when fiscal consolidation remains essential.

Table 8. **Social security finances**

Per cent of GDP

	1993	1994	1995	1996 Programme
Revenues	5.1	4.3	3.8	3.9
Expenditures	5.7	5.3	5.4	5.7
Deficit	–0.5	–1.1	–1.6	–1.9
Deficit financed by:				
Budget transfers	0.1	0.5	0.9	1.6
Borrowing requirement	–0.4	–0.6	–0.7	–0.2

Source: State Planning Organisation.

Towards a medium-term financial strategy

A number of scenarios for the evolution of the PSBR and the debt to GDP ratio over the next five years are presented in Annex II. Given the government's commitment to reduce money financing of the deficit, and the high interest rates needed to finance the PSBR, a primary public surplus will be needed to reduce the debt to GDP ratio over the next few years. Simulations presented in Annex II suggest that maintenance of a primary budget surplus of the targeted 2 per cent of GDP, over the next five years, could reduce the debt to GDP ratio from 48 per cent of GDP at the end of 1995 to 41 per cent by the year 2000. By contrast, maintaining a primary balance could result in a rising debt to GDP ratio, putting upward pressure on real interest-rates and increasing the risk that the government would ultimately resort to greater money financing of the deficit.

Since April 1994, limited access to international capital markets and a reduction in money finance have led to greater dependence on domestic borrowing to finance public deficits. However, lenders have demanded very large risk premia related to the uncertain real return on government paper. Inflation has been extremely volatile, with annual rates of consumer price inflation fluctuating between 78 and 130 per cent since January 1995. Such volatility has raised risk premia substantially, resulting in *ex post* real returns in the range of 30 to 45 per cent a year.

Inflation uncertainty has also restricted the maturities for new TL denominated debt, with the maturity structure proving highly sensitive to the ebb and flow of investor confidence in the government's financial strategy.[21] This has led to rapid turnover of the domestic debt stock; it has also posed problems due to uneven rates of turnover, particularly when average maturities have shortened.[22] Debt management could be made easier by issuing instruments that offer stronger guarantees of returns – either index-linked or floating rate paper. These would encourage domestic residents and Turkish banks to hold more longer-term funds in Turkish lira rather than in foreign currency instruments, thereby enabling the maturity structure of the domestic debt stock to be widened.

In principle, the problems of high *ex post* real borrowing costs and a volatile debt maturity structure could be alleviated by issuing index-linked government debt. The first problem arises because ex-ante uncertainty regarding inflation leads investors to demand substantial risk premia to insure against adverse outcomes. One feature of index-linked paper is that the government guarantees *ex post* real rates of return, hence substantially reducing or eliminating the risk premia related to inflation uncertainty. These premia are currently very large, implying substantial potential savings from such a strategy.

Turkey's very short average debt maturity is also a reflection of future inflation uncertainty, notably with respect to the timing and the degree to which the PSBR will be monetised. The problem here arises from the timing of any future inflation surprises, with the risk of a surprise increasing with lengthening maturities. Since index-linked paper eliminates the risks associated with unanticipated inflation, investors in them should *ceteris paribus* be more willing to hold longer maturities.

Although there are clear advantages to issuing index-linked debt, there are also technical problems. The first is what measure to use as an index. An obvious candidate is the State Institute of Statistics' consumer price index (CPI). There are two problems with this. The first question is one of timing. With comparatively high rates of inflation, real returns will be sensitive to the dates on which debt are issued and redeemed, as well as the dates on which the CPI samples are taken and calculated. Secondly, there is the question of which inflation measure is most appropriate for investors.[23] In addition, domestic prices include government administered prices, leaving the risk that the relevant index could be affected by delays in administered prices, with consequences for debt service. This risk would presumably result in a higher associated risk premium. However, such issues are less significant for longer term debt, as measures of inflation tend to converge over time.

An interesting alternative would be to index the rate of return on TL debt to the price of foreign exchange. This has the advantage that the exchange rate can be observed on the date of issue and redemption. However, since the market for Turkish lira is thin, a potential problem remains that a party might try to influence the exchange rate on a specific redemption date, leading to a premium to cover such a risk, as well as larger potential real exchange-rate movements.

Simulations based on plausible real interest rate assumptions suggest significant advantages in issuing index-linked TL government debt. These advantages clearly depend on inflation outcomes over the life of the debt. There is a break-even point at which the cost to the Treasury of issuing indexed debt or issuing non-indexed debt is identical. If inflation turns out lower than this, it is cheaper for the government to issue indexed-linked debt, and conversely if inflation is higher. A portfolio approach to risk-sharing would strongly favour issuing a mix of indexed and non-indexed debt, as is done by a number of OECD governments. Given the prohibitively high cost of issuing non-indexed debt at maturities of a year or more, this would suggest issuing index-linked debt for longer maturities, while continuing to issue shorter maturity non-indexed debt.

In summary, successful implementation of the 1996 budget is of critical importance. If this is realised, a number of further elements would be needed to restore medium-term fiscal balance:

- Turkey's debt service problem can only be tackled by keeping the primary public budget balance firmly in surplus. This will require continuing efforts to expand the tax base, to improve tax administration, and to tackle the financial problems of the SEEs and the social security organisations;
- assuming such action is taken, the ratio of debt service to GDP could decline rapidly in 1998 and beyond. The main contribution to this would be lower nominal interest rates, as inflation falls;
- if inflation outcomes are consistently better than those priced into non-indexed debt, issuing index-linked debt would lead to a substantially faster reduction in Turkey's debt service burden;
- the larger the proportion of index-linked debt, the greater the inflation risk borne by government. In the event of adverse inflation outcomes, this would increase the government's real debt service burden. This sharpens the incentive to achieve low inflation outcomes, but also implies a high cost if inflation is not reduced. Issuing a mix of index-linked and conventional debt instruments would diversify such risks, as well as providing a market-based indicator of monetary policy credibility.

Monetary and exchange rate policies

Monetary policy under high inflation

Inflation in Turkey has ratcheted-up over time[24] and has become deeply rooted (see Figure 8). High inflation has tended to reinforce the factors of

Figure 8. **INFLATION AND MONEY GROWTH**

Year-on-year growth rates

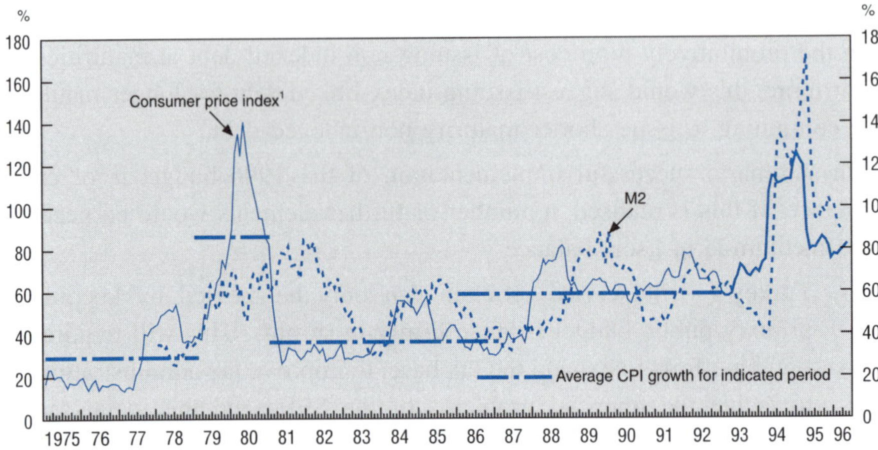

1. All items, urban population.

Source: Central Bank of Turkey and OECD, *Main Economic Indicators.*

instability that are at its origin: high fiscal deficits and their monetisation. The high inflation syndrome hinders rational fiscal management by disrupting the budgeting of expenditure, tax collection, and the market for public debt. The outcomes are high real interest rates, currency substitution, financial disintermediation, and greater instability in growth.[25] These developments have circumscribed the scope for pursuing anti-inflationary monetary policy.

High inflation has led to a progressive reduction in demand for cash balances and in the ratio of the monetary base to GDP. Such a decline has reduced the base of the inflation tax and thereby increased the inflationary impact of money creation to finance the deficit.[26] The authorities' capacity to tax cash balances is, however, limited in liberalised financial markets where residents can shift between domestic or foreign currency at low cost. The likely response to a perceived risk of higher inflation (taxation) is currency substitution. Each upward shift in inflation generates yet another decline in demand for cash balances and, beyond a certain point, seigniorage revenues actually decline. It is likely that current rates of inflation exceed those at which the maximum seigniorage revenue is attained.[27]

The authorities have also faced a decline in non-inflationary sources of finance. Financial intermediation has suffered a sustained decline since the mid-1980s (see Figure 9). Increased nominal uncertainty has led not only to a shortening of the maturity structure of debt instruments, but also to a shift towards greater use of foreign exchange as currency of denomination for contracts. Low or negative flows on external public debt[28] and the reduced scope of domestic financial markets have led to greater use of Central Bank financing of the deficit[29] (see Figure 10).

Shallow markets for public debt have strengthened the links between fiscal deficits and growth in the monetary aggregates. Not only has greater resort been made to monetisation, but the authorities' margin for manœuvre in the face of transitory shifts in financing requirements has also been reduced. Stop-go cycles in the Treasury's financing operations, partly in response to abrupt shifts in financial market sentiment, have resulted in unexpected shifts in the path for

Figure 9. **FINANCIAL DEEPENING**
As a percentage of GDP

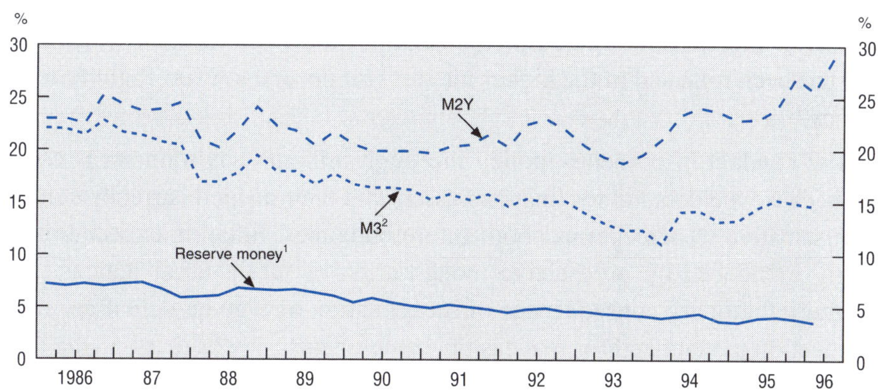

1. Reserve money is equal to the sum of currency issued, reserve balance of the banking sector, banking sector deposits and other items.
2. M3 is equal to M2Y minus foreign exchange deposits plus public sector deposits with banks plus other deposits with the Central Bank.

Source: Central Bank of Turkey.

Figure 10. **FISCAL DEFICITS AND SOURCES OF FINANCING**
As a percentage of GDP

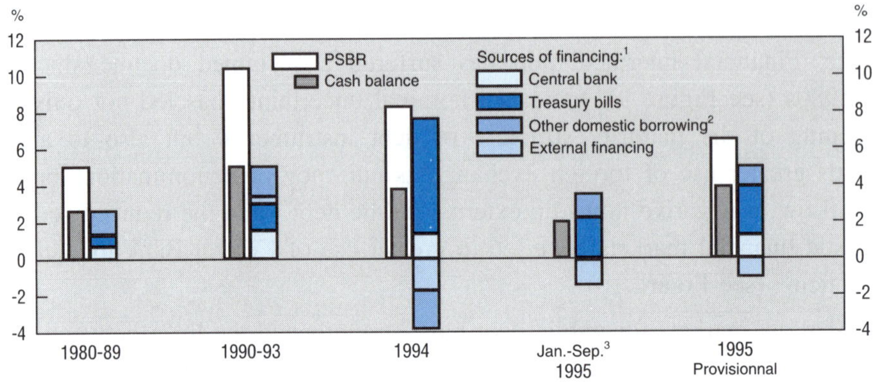

1. Sum of sources of financing equals consolidated budget's cash balance.
2. Including domestic borrowing net and other.
3. Cumulative figures to September 1995 divided by GDP for the whole year. Data on PSBR unavailable.

Source: State Planning Organisation, *Main Economic Indicators,* State Institute of Statistics, *Statistical Indicators 1923-1992,* and OECD.

prices, interest rates and the exchange rate. This occurred both in early 1994 and in late 1995 as the Treasury shifted from market financing of the deficit to Central Bank sources. If market participants extrapolate from past behaviour, their appraisal of the likelihood of similar shocks in future will increase. Such uncertainty has been reflected in the higher interest rate needed to avert flight to foreign currency.

The conduct of monetary policy in a high inflation environment is complicated because the demand for financial assets and their desired currency composition is sensitive to perceptions about future outcomes. Inflation expectations are strongly influenced by prospective monetisation of future fiscal deficits. However, the inflationary consequences of monetisation of a given deficit are in turn dependent on the demand for real cash balances. Thus, shocks that – in the eye of the public – may pose a further inflationary threat can lead to a contraction in real money demand which will in turn validate the expectations of higher inflation. Authorities may find such pressures difficult to resist, the more so when inflation expectations quickly feed into interest rates on domestic debt and a shortening of the maturity of new issues. Shocks to interest payments on public debt become another source of pressure on public sector finances and on money creation, reinforcing the feedback from inflation expectations to inflation outcomes.

Monetary and exchange rate developments

Monetary developments during 1995 were driven by the recovery from the 1994 financial crisis, as well as difficulties in pursuing stabilisation efforts. While growth in the monetary aggregates was consistently high, shifts in market sentiment and in the stance of policy led to sharply contrasting behaviour during the year. Monetary policy was initially set in the context of continuing stabilisation efforts which led the Central Bank to tighten policy in late 1994 in response to a rebound in inflation.[30] However, the outlook changed rapidly as economic prospects improved. In particular, improved confidence and high yields offered on domestic markets prompted renewed short-term capital inflows and a decline in currency substitution. Up to September 1995, the exchange rate was stronger than the stated objectives. Money growth accelerated, as strong reserve inflows overwhelmed Central Bank attempts to contain monetary expansion by means of sterilisation operations in thin markets. However, the outlook changed again following the September announcement of early elections for 24 December 1995. The ensuing shift in market sentiment and Treasury recourse to large scale Central Bank financing prompted a decline in international reserves and higher currency substitution (see Figure 11) as inflation and exchange rate uncertainty mounted. Despite this year-end setback, broad money and bank credit to the economy still recovered in 1995 and, with inflation coming down, there was an increase in real money balances. These gains are, however, likely to prove temporary unless the recent pick up in inflation is reversed.

The establishment of statutory limits on Central Bank advances to the Treasury was an important step forward towards establishing a more stable policy environment. The Central Bank law was modified in 1994 to introduce limits on the Central Bank advances account of the Treasury. The law sets the maximum share of an increase in total budgetary appropriations that can be financed by Central Bank advances. This percentage is set to decline over time, from 15 per cent in 1994, to 12 per cent in 1995, 10 per cent in 1996, 6 per cent in 1997, and 3 per cent thereafter.

As in 1994, monetary policy in 1995 was to make active use of interest rates to defend pre-specified ceilings on exchange rate depreciation and, thus, to

Figure 11. **CURRENCY SUBSTITUTION**

M2Y/M2

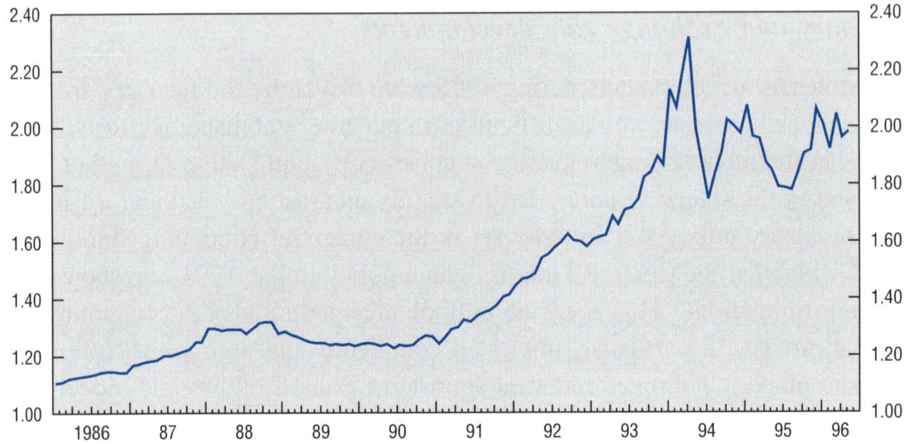

Source: Central Bank of Turkey.

achieve disinflation. This strategy had been followed because of unstable demand for domestic currency – which thwarts monetary targeting. The basic conditions necessary for a commitment to a nominal exchange rate anchor have similarly been lacking. While the basic strategy remained unchanged, policy implementation in 1995 was revised in the light of the previous year's experience, namely ambiguities with respect to base drift as the exchange rate proved to be stronger than expected following the April 1994 stabilisation programme.[31] In 1995, policy was set in terms of a crawling band for the exchange rate with the added condition that the ceiling to the exchange rate band was to be adjusted to assure that month-on-month movements in the exchange rate did not exceed the target inflation rate for the month.

Despite these technical adjustments, problems in monetary control re-emerged. The stabilisation programme envisaged a substantial decline in inflation to slightly below 40 per cent by December 1995, an increase in international reserves, and – in view of fiscal consolidation efforts – growth in reserve money[32] and Central Bank net domestic assets[33] of 65 per cent and 25 per cent respectively in the year to the last quarter of 1995 (see Table 9). In the event, reserve money expanded by over 80 per cent and, despite a significant decline, inflation remained some 25 percentage points above target. Net international reserves increased by $4.9 billion in the year to the last quarter of 1995, far exceeding its target value. Deviations between targets and outcomes were not as substantial for net domestic credit which grew by slightly under 25 per cent and finished the year 7.3 per cent above its limit, largely due to the fact that its fourth quarter 1994 level already exceeded the upper limit.

The evolution of both domestic and foreign Central Bank assets during 1995 was uneven, reflecting shifts in market confidence and in the stance of policy. Up to September, international reserves increased while net domestic assets contracted sharply as the Central Bank attempted to sterilise the monetary impact of reserve accumulation. In contrast, in the last quarter net domestic credit expanded by over 150 per cent and international reserves fell reflecting deteriorating financial market confidence as the Treasury made greater recourse to

Table 9. **Net domestic assets and net international reserves of the Central Bank: targets and outcomes**

	1994				1995			
	Q1	Q2	Q3	Q4	Q1	Q2	Q3	Q4
Levels								
Observed								
Net domestic assets (billion TL)	269 488	273 566	278 060	302 664	244 491	234 677	149 480	377 183
Net international reserves (million US dollar)	4 613	5 694	7 811	7 974	12 195	13 979	16 722	12 880
Targets								
Net domestic assets (billion TL)	269 488	305 258	294 529	292 995	259 862	269 223	333 996	366 296
Net international reserves (million US dollar)	4 613	4 263	4 913	5 613	10 497	11 960	10 766	10 350
Growth rates (quarter on quarter)								
Net domestic assets (in TL)		1.5	1.6	8.8	–19.2	–4.0	–36.3	152.3
Net international reserves (in US dollar)		23.4	37.2	2.1	52.9	14.6	19.6	–23.0

Source: Central Bank of Turkey, *Recent developments in Turkish economy*, March 1996.

Central Bank financing in the face of mounting difficulties in the placement of debt issues.

Recovery from the 1994 episode and pre-September 1995 developments

The period immediately following the outbreak of the 1994 financial crisis was dominated by very high interest rates, owing to macroeconomic uncertainty and strains on the banking system.[34] The gradual re-establishment of confidence during the first half of 1995 was reflected in a decline in the yield spread between Turkish securities and those offered in international markets. *Ex post* dollar returns from investing in the interbank market declined between 1994 and 1995 (see Figure 12). The announced policy of using the exchange rate as an instrument to further disinflation also contributed to strengthening investor confidence and encouraged a switch back into Turkish lira instruments.

The period up to September 1995 saw large capital inflows (mostly short-term) and a widespread shift back into TL instruments by residents (reverse currency substitution) on the back of improved financial market sentiment and still high returns offered on domestic securities, which were sustained by the strong pick-up in the real economy. The rate of depreciation slowed in response to strong capital inflows[35] and so did inflation. However, as capital inflows gained strength, the Central Bank undertook large scale purchases of foreign exchange that effectively prevented further strengthening of the exchange rate and led to a rapid accumulation of international reserves.[36] The impact of reverse currency substitution was somewhat damped as banks' open foreign exchange positions were reduced in response to tighter regulations.

As the monetary authorities' capacity to sterilise these inflows *via* open market operations was limited by the shallowness of the money market,[37] the first months of 1995 saw growth in the monetary aggregates at annualised rates of over 100 per cent. This expansion occurred despite reduced monetisation of fiscal deficits that underpinned the modest increase in domestic credit of the Central Bank[38] (see Table 10).

Nominal interest rates on TL denominated instruments declined between January and August 1995, along with the reduction in the risk premium and the strengthening of the exchange rate. Rates on 3-month Treasury bills fell from over 150 to below 90 per cent during this period. Real interest rates paid *ex post*

Figure 12. **REAL INTEREST RATES**
Annualised one week interbank rate

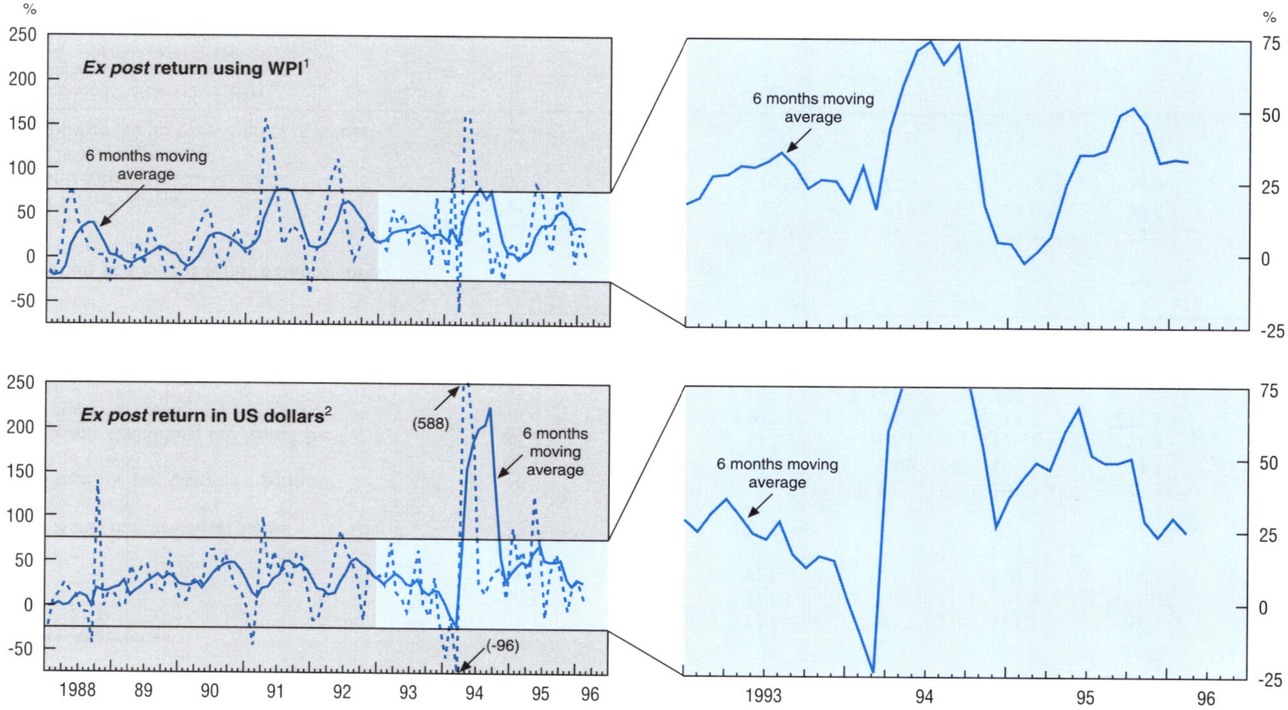

1. The *ex post* return is calculated using the end-of-period interest rate as the annual compound nominal rate minus the annualised monthly inflation rate.
2. The *ex post* return in US dollars is calculated as the annual compound nominal rate minus the rate of depreciation (at annual rate) over the following month.

Source: Central Bank of Turkey and OECD, *Main Economic Indicators*.

Table 10. **Monetary aggregates and Central Bank balance sheet items**

End of period data

	1992	1993	1994	1995	September 1995 [1]	December 1995 [2]	March 1996 [3]
	Annualised growth rates from previous period						
Monetary aggregates							
M2	61.1	59.6	120.1	97.7	111.5	61.6	63.1
M2Y	80.5	88.2	133.3	106.5	91.0	161.0	57.5
M3	65.0	47.4	123.1	102.4	119.7	58.2	79.4
Central Bank balance sheet items							
Reserve money							
Average for last quarter of period	68.8	63.3	88.0	82.3	101.3	35.3	37.6
End of period	67.1	68.8	82.6	84.9	109.2	27.7	52.4
Total assets (liabilities) of Central Bank	85.3	59.7	142.5	105.1	126.7	51.8	110.9
Total domestic credit	78.4	54.9	105.7	57.0	17.1	278.8	32.0
Foreign assets (in TL)	95.2	66.1	187.8	147.3	236.1	–1.4	168.0
Foreign assets (in US dollar)	16.1	–0.7	7.8	52.5	138.8	–60.2	50.5
	Per cent						
Composition of Central Bank balance sheet							
Share in total assets							
Foreign assets	43.1	44.8	53.2	64.2	71.5	64.2	68.1
Net foreign assets [4]	11.5	12.1	–2.2	30.5	43.0	30.5	35.4
Cash credit to public sector	32.5	38.0	30.9	32.8	24.1	32.8	33.0
Share in monetary base							
Liabilities due to open market operations	23.2	14.9	3.2	12.0	23.7	12.0	9.0

1. September 1995/December 1994.
2. December 1995/September 1995.
3. March 1996/December 1995.
4. Defined as net foreign assets divided by net foreign assets plus domestics assets. Average for last month of period.

Source: Central Bank of Turkey, *Monthly Statistical Bulletin.*

by domestic borrowers followed a different pattern: they were negative towards the end of 1994 and then rose sharply. This pattern was brought about by developments in both financial markets and in the real exchange rate. Initially, the fall in *ex post* dollar returns between 1994 and early 1995 combined with strong real exchange rate appreciation (*i.e.* a slower rate of depreciation than the rate of inflation) led to a sharp drop in real TL interest rates in early 1995. Thereafter, as real appreciation levelled-off, falling inflation brought about a sharp increase in *ex post* TL real rates of return (see Figure 12). Two factors helped to sustain such high levels of real interest rates: the Treasury's shift towards market sources of financing the PSBR and renewed private sector demand for credit.

Bank credit recovered from its 1994 setback as the economic expansion gathered strength, in line with a normalisation of banking conditions (see Figure 13). After large repayments of foreign obligations in 1994, which forced banks to raise additional funds on the domestic market, pressures on bank funding costs eased somewhat. As the increase in the total supply of funds was

Figure 13. **BANK CLAIMS IN REAL TERMS**[1]

Index January 1993 = 100

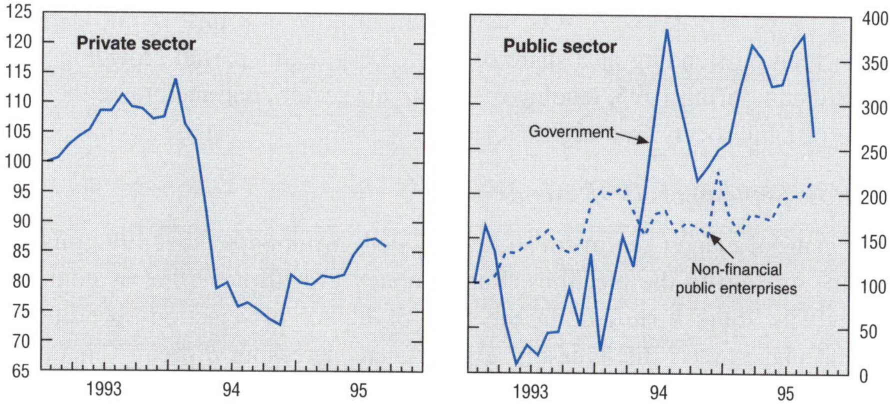

1. Figures on bank claims have been deflated by the consumer price index (all items, urban population).

Source: Central Bank of Turkey and OECD, *Main Economic Indicators.*

Figure 14. **BANKING SECTOR CLAIMS ON PUBLIC AND PRIVATE SECTOR**[1]

Share in GDP

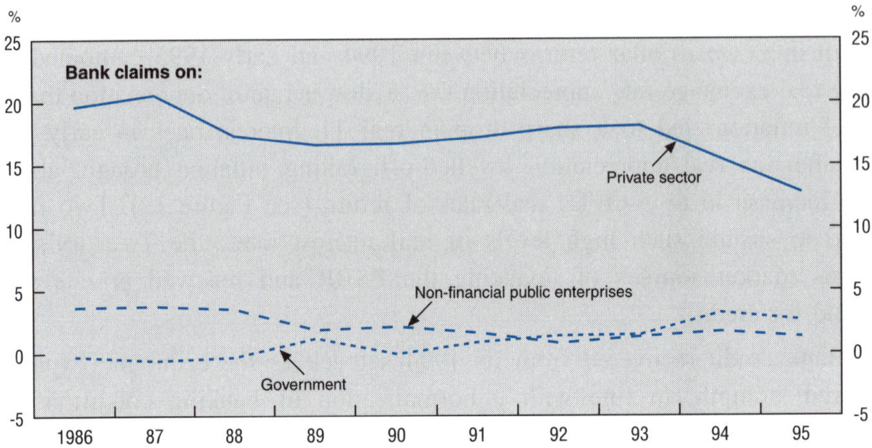

1. Excluding Central Bank. Last observation: Q3 1995.
Source: Central Bank of Turkey.

largely absorbed by increases in Treasury issues, the recovery in real bank lending to the private sector was insufficient to prevent a further fall in private sector credit outstanding as a share of GDP. Despite this partial crowding-out of private credit during 1995, lending to the private sector continued to be the major source of bank assets (see Figure 14).

Post-September 1995 trends

Financial market sentiment shifted radically from September 1995 onwards, with the lead-up to the elections. Rapid money growth nevertheless continued, although its sources shifted. In the face of higher pre-election spending and political uncertainty, the Treasury experienced increasing difficulty in funding the PSBR and made renewed recourse to Central Bank financing.[39] Not surprisingly, Treasury bill maturities shortened considerably, interest rates rose sharply, and the exchange rate also weakened significantly, reflecting renewed currency substitution and a reversal of capital flows.

From November onwards, the Central Bank began quoting forward foreign exchange rates to stabilise markets, and to provide direction with respect to near term future rates. Sales of foreign exchange, including forward sales, resulted in a drop of some $4.3 billion in reserves in November and December. Returns on TL instruments (measured either in real terms or in terms of US dollars) nonetheless remained high during the last quarter, despite the depreciation/inflation shock and diminished pressure from both Treasury financing operations and open market operations by the Central Bank.

Political uncertainty remained unabated after the inconclusive December election results. To date, the authorities have made limited, albeit fragile progress in restoring financial market stability. While the Treasury made ample use of Central Bank advances in January,[40] a subsequent shift to market sources of financing allowed repayment of part of these advances.[41] The exchange rate, after experiencing a decline of some 12 per cent in December, depreciated at a somewhat more steady pace during the first quarter of 1996 and by early-July 1996 rates on Treasury bills had fallen to some 120 per cent, compared with the peak rates of 240 per cent on 3-month paper in January. The Treasury has been able to issue debt with maturities up to seven months, foreign reserves have been partially restored, and growth of the monetary aggregates, albeit remaining very high, has moderated. But foreign currency substitution remains near historic highs, undoubtedly reflecting the state of financial market confidence.

The 1995 policy dilemma in retrospect

Developments during the first part of 1995 made it increasingly unlikely that targets for inflation and monetary expansion would be met. The authorities' decision to intervene in the exchange market to resist faster-than-desired real appreciation brought about higher-than-programmed monetary expansion and higher inflation. With the benefit of hindsight, an alternative strategy might have been to accept less rapid exchange rate depreciation and a more limited degree of reserve accumulation in early 1995[42] so that inflation would have been lower. To be sure, such a strategy would have had risks, notably a loss of competitiveness and a larger current account deficit. It would have left the authorities in a weaker foreign reserve position with which to face the renewed pressures arising from currency substitution towards the end of the year (barely a year after a severe run on the Turkish lira). Nonetheless, a decision to let the real exchange rate appreciate further would have strengthened the disinflation pressures at a critical stage of the stabilisation process.

Policies for 1996

Unforeseeable events have introduced delays and required revisions to policy announcements for 1996. A period of uncertainty linked to extended negotiations to form a coalition government delayed approval of the 1996 budget until April. The setting of monetary policy has been formulated in line with the 1996 budget; in particular, it incorporates an underlying inflation assumption of 69 per cent. The policy framework sets a target for growth in net domestic assets; its growth should be significantly below the inflation target. In addition, the Central Bank will monitor growth in reserve money and help to sustain stability in foreign exchange markets. Thus, policy has shifted away from active use of the exchange rate in the strategy to reduce inflation. It is therefore foreseeable that the stability in real exchange rate observed in the first months of 1996 will continue. The Central Bank has stressed the importance of further progress on fiscal consolidation in order to attain inflation objectives.

Prospects for monetary policy

Finding a way out of the high inflation maze is not straightforward. Past experience suggests that there is no single most successful strategy, and country experiences vary. It is unlikely that a detailed strategy to regain monetary stability can be spelled-out in advance as management of short-term pressures and stabilisation of volatile expectations take on an inordinate importance. Policy precommitments could help to accelerate the disinflation process and ease the burden of adjustment. However, the authorities must be committed and able to deliver such commitments.

Attempts to establish nominal anchors and/or to pre-commit government policies[43] are likely to fail as a medium-term strategy for monetary stability, unless the underlying fundamentals have been sufficiently strengthened. Exchange-rate anchors and/or incomes policies have played an important role in disinflation episodes around the world, but they have only been successful in accelerating the disinflation process once structural measures have been taken. Use of an exchange rate anchor is risky in the current context. A failure to sustain policy announcements might bring about a quick loss of market confidence with possible systemic consequences. Likewise, targeting of monetary aggregates lacks credibility when the Central Bank cannot control its own balance sheet. Turkish experience shows that the control of the Central Bank's balance sheet faces severe difficulties due to both fiscal pressures, as well as large volatile movements associated with currency substitution and capital flows.

Prospects for fiscal consolidation remain uncertain. Even so, in the short to medium term, clarification of the government's monetary strategy is needed, as volatility in money markets and the exchange rate can impose heavy costs on public finances and on the economy as a whole. Given the difficulties in establishing a medium-term policy anchor, an interim strategy – while further progress on structural reform is being made – might be useful to provide some indication of the expected pace of monetary expansion and to improve market confidence in near term policies. Announcement of policy intentions and commitments to intermediate targets[44] could also play a role in day-to-day management and help to reduce uncertainty about the near term outlook.

Steady reductions in the statutory limits to Central Bank advances to the Treasury take on a special importance in this context. This is an important step in making Treasury operations more predictable, but it does not establish a sufficiently firm anchor for expectations regarding monetary expansion. First, the nominal amount of the ceiling on Central Bank advances is set as a ratio of an increase in budgetary appropriations, but the latter is subject to revision during the year. Second, as the 1995 experience shows, even if overall Central Bank advances for the year are maintained, uncertainty can still exist regarding the timing of the Treasury's funding operations. Finally, net domestic credit can be expanded by other means, such as open market purchases of private or public debt instruments. In sum, further pre-commitments of policy intentions would substantially help to clarify the monetary policy outlook.

Gaining a greater margin of manœuvre requires strengthening the financial position of both the Central Bank and the banking system. The improvement in the Central Bank's foreign exchange risk ratio to close to 1.1 during 1995[45] is an important development and further moves in this direction are needed. The Central Bank has also gained greater control of its balance sheet as direct lending operations to public bodies have been suspended. Furthermore, some of its assets – including a large part of the revaluation account with the Treasury – have been converted into securities which can be useful for the conduct of open market operations. The development of open market operations has provided the Central Bank with a direct means to influence market liquidity, but it continues to be a net debtor in this market – a factor that may limit its ability to control market liquidity.

Interactions between inflation outcomes and monetisation of deficits complicate policy formulation, but they may also become part of a virtuous circle once public sector finances are brought on to firmer ground. Expectations of an improved fiscal outlook are likely to raise the demand for domestic currency and to diminish pressures on Central Bank domestic credit expansion, thereby providing more room for manœuvre for monetary policy. However, as the experience of 1995 shows, problems in monetary control will remain even when market expectations improve, if fiscal pressures remain unabated. Furthermore, temporary gains on the stabilisation front will quickly disappear if the authorities do not have the means to deal with temporary set-backs such as those encountered in the last quarter of 1995. Building confidence in medium-term outcomes and strengthening the financial positions of the Treasury and the Central Bank to resist short-term pressures would be important elements in establishing the pre-conditions for a successful stabilisation strategy.

The banking and financial system

The upswing in economic activity in 1995 helped the banking system to recover from its early 1994 set back (see Figure 15). After large repayment of foreign obligations in 1994, which created additional pressure on banks to raise funds on the domestic market, pressures on banks' funding costs have eased. Fears of a full fledged banking crisis have faded and banks have balanced their foreign currency exposure somewhat. Credit to the private sector recovered and the position of the banking system improved. However, deep-seated impediments to financial deepening remain and, in a longer term perspective, a number of reforms will be needed to foster development of a sound financial system. The current structure of the Turkish banking system is summarised in Box 1.

Levels of financial intermediation in Turkey are low by international standards and have fallen further in recent years. As shown in the bottom panel of Figure 16, the ratio of broad money to GDP tends to be higher in countries with higher per capita income. Financial deepening in Turkey remains below what

Figure 15. **GROWTH IN REAL BANK CLAIMS ON THE PRIVATE SECTOR**[1]

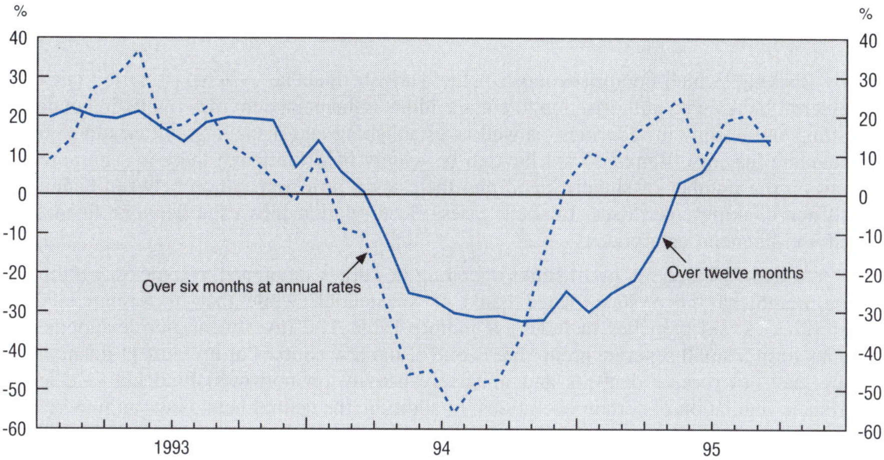

1. Figures on bank claims have been deflated by the consumer price index (all items, urban population).
Source: Central Bank of Turkey and OECD, *Main Economic Indicators.*

would be expected according to this relationship. Inflation also has a strong influence on levels of financial intermediation (the top panel of Figure 16).

The high inflation syndrome has taxed financial development heavily. The inflation tax has lowered desired cash balances and high nominal uncertainty has acted as a deterrent to contracting in domestic currency. Currency substitution has taken place on a large scale. Nearly one-half of banks' deposits are denominated in foreign exchange and so are a large share of their loans. As a result, domestic securities markets remain thin, a factor that constrains public debt management. Access to TL-denominated credit by firms is also limited.

Loans offered by Turkish banks are normally short term (the average maturity is some 4 months) and banks play a minor role in investment finance. In the case of large projects, which represent a substantial volume of investment flows, the firms involved are large and in many cases have access to sources of finance abroad sometimes at better terms than the banks themselves. At the same time most small firms are not seen as credit-worthy by banks or have access to preferential credit from state-owned banks.

Box 1. **Structure of the Turkish banking system**

Banking, which comprises most of the Turkish financial system, is carried out by universal banks with authorisation to engage in most financial activities (including underwriting and trading in securities, as well as establishing and managing mutual funds, but excluding leasing). Banks do not have to be widely held (although there is a minimum limit on the number of shareholders) and there is no strict separation between banking and non-banking enterprises. In some cases, close relationships exist between financial and non-financial enterprises.

At end-1995, equity of all banks operating in Turkey amounted to some $6.1 billion. The weight of the 5 state-owned banks is substantial, while that of foreign banks (subsidiaries and branches included) is minor (Table 11). Investment and development banks form a small separate group that is one of the few sources of investment financing; they may not receive deposits and must rely heavily on borrowed fund but face less stringent regulation of certain operations. In addition, the central bank plays an important role in the intermediating of funds as lender to the Treasury and as recipient of foreign currency deposits from nationals living abroad.*

Establishment of new banks, following liberalisation measures in the 1980s, has fostered competition. The banking system is not highly concentrated as the 4 largest banks account for slightly over 1/3 of total equity and the largest bank represents about 14 per cent of total equity of the banking system. In addition there are a number of fairly small private banks (17 out of 31 have a paid-in capital that represents less than 2 per cent of the system's equity) which probably do not reach the economies of scale and scope necessary to carry out full-fledged banking operations efficiently.

Branch networks are not highly developed and these are owned mostly by the state-owned banks. This reflects only in part the larger size of state-owned banks as even older larger private banks tend to have a higher ratio of assets per branch. State-owned banks tend to have stronger ties with non-financial public enterprises and several of them were established for specific purposes such as financing small enterprises, agriculture or real estate development.

* Foreign exchange deposits of residents abroad stood at 16 per cent of total domestic liabilities of the Central Bank at end-1995. These deposits correspond to the Dresdner Bank scheme, according to which a foreign bank acts as an agent of the Central Bank in collecting deposits from Turkish workers abroad. Turkish commercial banks are also active in this field.

Access to credits denominated in foreign exchange, which account for close to half of all bank claims, is limited to exporting firms. Increased currency substitution may have accentuated the bias towards export-related finance. In

Table 11. **The Turkish banking system**

	Number of banks	Size distribution (share in total)		Capitalisation ratios			Return on assets			Return on capital			Past due loans[1] (as share of total credits at year-end)		
		Assets	Equity	1993 Dec.	1994 Dec.	1995 Dec.	1993	1994	1995 Sep.	1993	1994	1995 Sep.	1993	1994	1995
Deposit banks															
State-owned banks	5	38.1	21.5	14.9	8.1	8.9	3.0	0.3	1.0	37.4	–1.8	10.2	4.6	4.7	4.7
Private banks	31	51.4	65.3	9.1	9.7	14.2	4.4	4.1	4.9	42.5	43.5	35.4	1.9	2.7	2.1
Foreign banks	19	3.9	6.5	13.1	20.2	22.9	7.3	16.7	11.4	44.0	70.7	55.3	3.9	11.1	3.1
Development and investment banks	14	6.5	6.7	11.0	3.6	9.4	1.5	–0.8	3.8	9.2	–36.9	64.6	4.4	8.9	9.2
Total banking sector	69	100.0	100.0	11.0	8.9	12.6	3.7	2.5	3.5	38.0	31.7	32.3	3.1	4.4	2.9

1. Include credits to all residents and non-residents, including credits to other financial institutions.
Source: Central Bank of Turkey.

Figure 16. **FINANCIAL DEEPENING IN TURKEY AND OTHER COUNTRIES**

Average 1990-94

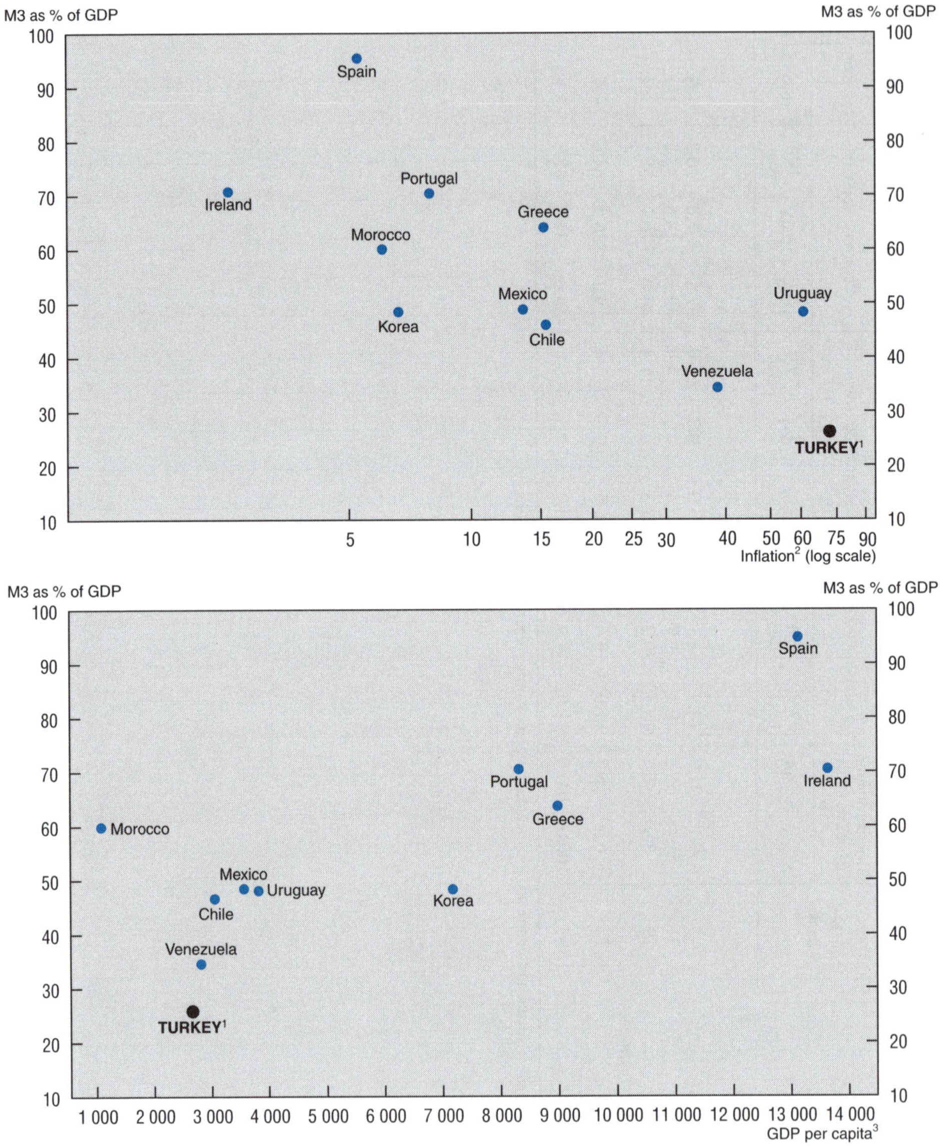

1. M2Y.
2. Measured by the growth of the consumer price index.
3. At current prices and current exchange rates.

Source: IMF, *International Financial Statistics*, and OECD, *National Accounts*.

1995, export loans accounted for some 35 per cent of all non-preferential credits, up from some 25 per cent in the years preceding the 1994 crisis.

Average returns on assets and on capital are high by international standards (see Figure 17). Large differentials between deposit and lending rates reflect only in part large bank profits, as other factors, such as required reserves and taxes, also play a major role (see OECD, 1994). High reported profits are, however, somewhat overstated, as reported net interest income does not make allowances for loss of purchasing power of bank assets due to inflation.

Bank capitalisation ratios went up as a result of improvement in the banks' net income during 1995. The average for the risk-weighted capital ratio at end-1995 was 12.6 per cent, a substantial improvement from 1994 levels (see Box 1). However, this aggregate figure hides wide disparities among groups of banks. Public sector banks are the group with the lowest capitalisation ratios and the smallest improvement since 1994; they have not yet regained their 1993 levels.

In 1995 one bank was privatised and further progress in this area is likely to bring about efficiency gains and greater competition.[46] In several cases these banks may not be entirely adapted to commercial banking operations since they were established with a specific purpose and have special functions defined in their by-laws. In this context, it would be helpful to draw a clear separation between normal banking activities and those undertaken as part of public policy. Such a move would increase transparency both in public sector accounts and in banks' financial statements.

Banks' balance sheets have also been strengthened by the decline in open foreign exchange positions – reflecting tighter regulations – and by a decline in the share of past-due loans from 4.4 per cent of all loans in 1994 to 2.9 per cent in 1995. While provisioning for past-due loans has been maintained (provisioning covers some 69 per cent of past-due credits), the largest problem in this area seems to be under-reporting of non-performing assets due to the fact that loan-losses are not deductible for tax purposes unless the loan is under legal follow-up.

The recovery in the banking system is a positive development that should remove a major constraint on the expansion of bank credit to the economy. However, the trend decline in financial intermediation over recent years suggests

Figure 17. **COST OF DEPOSITS TO BANKS AND BANKS' LENDING MARGINS**

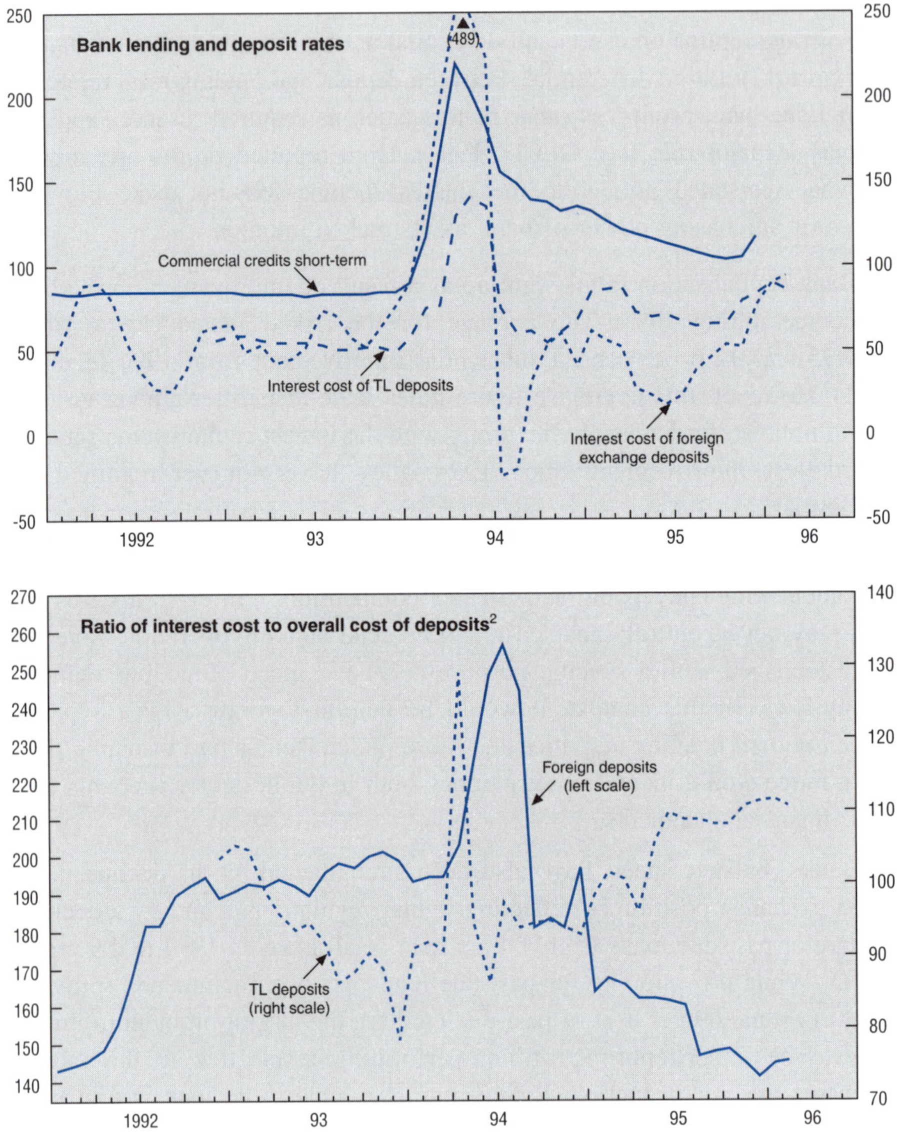

1. Including realised exchange rate depreciation.
2. Overall cost of deposits includes interest cost and cost of required reserves and liquidity requirements.
Source: Central Bank of Turkey.

deeper seated impediments to the development of the financial system which, thereby, act as a deterrent on growth. First and foremost is the underlying macroeconomic environment and the unpredictability of government financial policies. A second element is the regulatory environment. In this regard, there is an important role for policies to foster competition, to reduce the regulatory burden on banks, and to improve the supervisory and prudential framework necessary to providing appropriate incentives.

Declining financial intermediation has occurred despite financial liberalisation measures undertaken in the 1980s.[47] While the decline does not appear to be the outcome of "financial repression", there is further scope for liberalisation: banks face high liquidity and reserve requirements and a large portion of the banking system is state-owned.

Prudential supervision

Financial regulation and prudential supervision play an important role in creating an incentive structure that is conducive to safe and sound banking and maintenance of the public's confidence in the banking system. Market discipline is enhanced when bank owners reap the benefits from sound banking operations and bear the burden of bad decisions. Thus, adequate capitalisation is key to ensuring that proper incentives remain in place. Another important factor in maintaining market discipline are decisions by large depositors and bond holders. To be effective, this mechanism requires that returns to investors be related to their capacity to appraise financial strength and management of the banks. Disclosure requirements play an important role in this context. While lender of last resort measures and deposit insurance systems may be needed to limit the risk perceived by small and/or non-sophisticated investors, it should be recalled that early corrective action is preferable to costly remedial measures. In the end, the most effective policies are those directed towards reinforcing the incentive structure faced by all parties involved.

Overall measures to strengthen the supervisory authorities' capacity for early corrective action and capacity for monitoring are, thus, needed. Perhaps the key requirement is to generate transparency and certainty regarding the steps to be taken both by the bank and the authorities as the financial condition of a bank deteriorates or when non-compliance with financial regulations occurs.

Since 1994 several steps have been taken to improve financial regulation and simplification of administrative procedures (such as elimination of a prior authorisation requirement for opening of additional branches). The more substantive steps are changes in line with harmonisation with European Union regulations and pertain to consolidated supervision, rules to encourage asset diversification (including *inter alia* limits on personal loans and limits on holdings of real estate and investments), and minimum capital requirements. However, substantial progress can still be made in several areas: consolidated supervision does not cover all subsidiaries of banks, and current limits on large exposures and related lending may still leave room for substantial concentration of bank risk and possible conflicts of interest.

Accounting standards were revised in 1986, external auditors have been required since 1987, and publication of audited financial statements is now a requirement. However, these standards do not include provisions regarding inflation accounting and this is a major impediment in attaining greater transparency in bank accounts.

Deposit insurance was extended to all savings deposits in domestic and foreign currency following the 1994 crisis.[48] At the time, public confidence was eroded as losses on foreign exchange positions led to failure of three small banks. Each bank must pay a fee to the Savings Deposit Fund that varies according to the amount of insured deposits and its capitalisation level. However, this may not provide a strong enough incentive to counterbalance the moral hazard problems to which the system is currently exposed.

Another area for improvement in prudential regulation concerns banks' open foreign exchange positions which may place both their own funds and depositors' savings at risk. Banks have taken on substantial open foreign exchange positions to lower their funding costs. However, as the 1994 experience shows, this strategy carries risks not only for the individual bank involved but also for the system as a whole since the Central Bank's capacity to act as a lender of last resort is constrained when a substantial share of banking operations takes place in foreign currency. Following the banking crisis, regulations were tightened and banks are now allowed to have open net positions of at most 50 per cent of their capital base. For the purposes of the calculation of this limit, assets and liabilities indexed to foreign exchange have a 50 per cent weight. Regulations establish an exemption for five investment banks, three of which are state-owned.

Regulation of market risks calls for stricter limits or a larger capitalisation requirement for operations in which a bank faces larger risk. On these grounds, an argument can be made that tighter regulation is called for in Turkey than in countries with more stable exchange rates. Compared with regulations in many other OECD countries, Turkish regulations appear to be more lax. Another important step is for bank regulators to place greater emphasis on the quality of banks' internal methods for risk evaluation and control as a prerequisite for authorisation to deal in instruments that carry market risk. Regular assessments of such internal control methods should form part of the prudential framework.

III. Accelerating structural transformation: The role of the Seventh Five Year Plan and Customs Union with the EU

A root cause of large fiscal deficits and persistently high inflation has been the lack of progress in certain key areas of reform. Two recent events could, however, impart renewed impetus to structural reform: the preparation of the seventh Five Year Plan and the entry into the customs union agreement with the European Union. The new Plan provides an overall framework for needed structural changes and their blueprints. The customs union will stimulate structural transformation by strengthening competitive forces in the economy and modernising Turkey's legal framework (*inter alia*, for protection of intellectual property rights and policies against anti-competitive behaviour) through harmonisation with EU legislation. Faster structural reform is a necessary condition for reaping maximum benefits from the customs union arrangements. This part of the Survey first discusses the new Five Year Plan from a strategic point of view. It then assesses various implications of the customs union with the EU.

The Seventh Five Year Plan for 1996-2000

The Seventh Five Year Plan (which was delayed one year due to the 1994 foreign exchange crisis) was presented to Parliament in 1995. The latest Plan lays out ambitious targets for transforming Turkey's human and physical resource base into one able to support a modern, more market-oriented economy over the period 1996-2000.[49] Previous Plans typically became obsolete soon after their preparation as their macroeconomic underpinnings became detached from reality. What distinguishes the new Plan from the previous ones is the emphasis it puts on various reforms necessary for the structural transformation of the Turkish economy. The new Plan hence provides an overall framework for a comprehensive structural reform programme. It presents a blueprint with detailed quantitative goals for human resource development, agricultural and industrial output, science and technology outcomes, as well as guidelines for reforming regulatory control, the tax and social security systems, the core public sector, the judicial and security services, public infrastructure, regional economic development policies and environmental protection standards.

The Plan's macroeconomic targets are for GDP growth of between 5.0 and 6.6 per cent per annum over the coming five years; and as population growth is projected to be some 1.6 per cent per annum, per capita income would grow at some 3½ to 5 per cent a year. An on-going primary budget surplus of 3 per cent of GDP is projected to contribute to lowering the overall PSBR to some 3 per cent of GDP by the year 2000. And this, combined with a tighter monetary policy and accelerated structural reform, is projected to bring inflation down to around 6 to 8 per cent by the year 2000 and to hold the current account deficit at a small percentage of GDP. Simultaneously achieving these macroeconomic growth and inflation targets (by the year 2000) would probably represent the most successful economic adjustment in post-war Turkish history. Realising these targets would be an enormous step towards putting the economy onto a sustainable medium-term growth path, with manageable public finances and single digit inflation. (The OECD's medium-term baseline presented in Annex II illustrates what would need to be done in terms of key fiscal parameters to achieve the Plan's output and inflation goals).

There is little controversy that large and persisting fiscal imbalances and high inflation have their roots in the slow pace of public sector reform. As in many developing countries, the Turkish public sector played a dominant early role as a provider of basic commercial goods and services (other than public goods), owing to private sector limitations. Indeed, the SEEs played a critical role in Turkey's rapid and successful industrialisation and economic development. But the undoubted dynamism and maturity of the private sector, as Turkey enters customs union with the EU, clearly shows that the need for this transitional stage of "state capitalism" was passed some time ago. Despite this, reform of the bloated, inefficient public sector has severely lagged over the last ten years. And this slippage probably goes far in explaining the difficulties in meeting the targets for basic education, health and other social goals[50] set five years earlier.

The last decade reveals a record of slow and patchy progress. First, tax revenue has risen slowly but steadily to some 18.1 per cent of GDP in 1995; but this has been insufficient to fund adequate provision of public goods (notably public education and health) because of a heavy debt-service burden. Efforts to widen the tax base have centred on improving administration through computerisation, issuing individual tax numbers and more extensive auditing. Despite substantial improvement in tax collection, coverage and tax assessment of the unregistered economy remains problematic. In 1995, indirect tax represented over 60 per cent of total tax revenue. Although horizontal tax equity has been improved, such heavy reliance on indirect tax has added to Turkey's already skewed primary income distribution.[51]

Second, in the absence of significant steps, the financial position of the social security institutions has deteriorated substantially; despite the young average age of the population, the social security system received subsidies of some 1.5 per cent of GDP in 1995. This deficit reflects very low collection rates and late payments (in the face of high inflation) as well as one of the world's lowest statutory retirement ages. A bill to phase in higher retirement ages over a 10 year period (to 55 years for women, 60 for men) and to raise minimum contribution to 7 400 and 9 000 premium days respectively was presented, but not passed before the dissolution of Parliament at the end of 1995.

Third, progress has been slow in restructuring SEEs and closing large loss-making SEEs. Reform of the SEEs remains a central plank of the structural programme. SEEs deficits have been reduced from around 2½ per cent of GDP in 1993, to an estimated 0.8 per cent in 1995. In 1994, as part of the IMF stand-by agreement, the losses of the largest SEEs were monitored and some loss makers were to be restructured, sold or closed. Seven enterprises were scheduled to be closed at the end of 1994. In the event, only a few small enterprises were actually closed, although activity in the others was scaled back extensively. Planned closure of the large loss making KARDEMIR iron and steel complex was cancelled. The government eventually assumed all past debt and the assets were handed over to the workers and local residents for 1 lira.[52]

Fourth, only slow progress has been made in reactivating the long delayed privatisation programme. From 1985 to 1994, a few firms were sold, and there were also block sales of government-owned shares in some companies, with cumulative receipts of $2.3 billion. For 1995 the government's original target for privatisation was based on 20 projects. Due to legal delays, the target was steadily reduced from $5 billion to $2.4 billion, and subsequently to $1.3 billion. In the event, revenue amounted to some $574 million in 1995, although some of the least attractive companies in the Privatisation Agency's portfolio (*e.g.* the dairies and slaughter houses) were sold.[53]

Finally, reform of agricultural support has made little progress. Turkey's producer subsidy equivalent (PSE) is estimated to have been 34 per cent in 1994, marginally lower than the OECD average, but still above levels prevailing in Turkey before 1991. Subsidies to agriculture were raised significantly prior to the 1995 elections, underlining the close connection between political pressures and agricultural support.[54]

What can be done to speed up reform?

The reasons for slow progress in reform are complex, but probably reflect the ability of special interest groups to block reform in a fragmented and highly competitive political system. In the absence of strong external competition or an external crisis, this situation has often led to political gridlock and the inability to find co-operative solutions which would benefit the community as a whole.[55]

Given the lack of transparency and the degree of cross subsidisation of economic activity, most Turkish citizens are probably ignorant of the very high dead-weight costs of government intervention. Hence, exposing such costs through an independent body (such as the Australian Industries Commission) could play a useful role in informing public opinion, building a constituency for reform, as well as enhancing government accountability.[56]

To illustrate this point, while a handful of SEEs undoubtedly perform efficiently (*e.g.* Petkim and Eregli Iron and Steel), the enormous waste and inefficiency in other public sector enterprises largely escapes public scrutiny. Although substantial progress has been made in recent years, a striking example of cross subsidisation is that losses in the state coal mines, per worker (in 1992) were equivalent to six times per capita national income.[57] Further, the explicit operating subsidies of State Economic Enterprises (SEEs) were equivalent to around 50 per cent of the central government's education budget and 300 per cent of its health budget over the period 1978-91.[58] Indeed, a rough estimate of other deadweight costs (*i.e.* access to subsidised credit, preferences in government procurement and overmanning[59]) could easily double the above figures.[60]

The need to set priorities

Despite the burden of inefficiencies in the public sector[61] and chronic inflation, medium-term growth prospects are good, owing to a dynamic private sector. But this favourable outlook risks being eroded. Unless underlying fiscal imbalances are quickly addressed within a coherent medium-term strategy, the economy risks perpetuating the boom-bust cycles of the past. This would be in marked contrast to the need to converge towards the EU "low-inflation norm". Continuing economic instability could also deter inflows of foreign direct investment, a vital element in ensuring the success of customs union with the EU.

The 1995 Five Year Plan did not set a specific hierarchy of priorities, although it does recognise the necessity for downsizing the public sector to free the resources necessary for enhanced human capital development. It would, of course, be desirable to make rapid progress across as broad a front of reforms as possible.[62] But given the glacial pace of reform over the past decade – with the notable exception of the passage of the EU customs union agreement – achieving better results in the future will demand abandonment of the previous practice of pursuing an agenda without a clear set of priorities.

Given the scarcity of administrative and bureaucratic resources, more effective outcomes would probably be obtained if reform focused on implementing EU customs union and on a limited programme of high priorities, especially those elements which contribute to strengthening public finances and controlling inflation; have the maximum impact in exposing special interest groups to domestic and foreign competition and hence in building a constituency for reform; and increase the transparency and accountability of government for its actions.

Drawing on the experience of some of the successful reforming countries as well as Turkey's latest Five Year Plan, the OECD Secretariat's priority list comprises two categories of actions. The first category includes those which would provide the fiscal savings needed to fund greater investment in human capital and reform elsewhere and in this sense are more urgently required:

- widening the tax base by allocating more resources more effectively to tax administration and auditing, as well as levying heavier financial sanctions for late payment and/or under-reporting;
- restructuring or liquidating large loss-making SEEs to enforce hard budget constraints and to raise productivity – thereby paving the way to promoting the stalled privatisation programme;
- improve effective social security collection rates; steadily raise the retirement age to put the social security system on to a sounder actuarial basis, as a transition towards greater dependency on private pensions.

The second category would then include:

- exploiting the opportunity of EU customs union to expose the economy to greater competition through vigorous application of competition laws and deregulation[63] (including agriculture);
- accelerating the development of human capital through raising compulsory schooling from five to eight years (or beyond) as soon as feasible, by providing more (and better) financial and teaching resources;
- improving basic universal health care facilities and adopting a fundamental reform of the social security system (see Box 2);
- addressing pressing public infrastructure needs, particularly the concerns about unstable electricity supply; and
- strengthening prudential control of financial institutions.

Legislation in some of these areas (*e.g.* competition policy, pension reform, introduction of the special consumption tax) has already been presented to Parliament or is awaiting implementation, but action remains slow.[64]

EU customs union: a challenge and an opportunity

The EU is Turkey's largest export market and source of foreign supply (representing around 50 per cent of Turkish exports and imports in 1995). Turkey entered into customs union with the European Union on 1 January 1996,

Box 2. **Social security reform**

The provision of social security in Turkey is in need of urgent reform. The financial position of the social security institutions is deteriorating rapidly, largely due to a bankrupt pension system. The International Labour Office estimates that current arrangements could result in the deficit of the pension system rising from 1.8 per cent of GDP in 1995 to 5.7 per cent of GDP in 2020.

The roots of the problem are an exceptionally low retirement age and incoherent contribution levels relative to benefits – exacerbated by low premium collection rates. Under the current system, male contributors to the scheme are eligible for pension after 25 working years, females after only 20 years. Most individuals can qualify for pension in their early forties. While pension benefit is low (around 35 per cent of national average earnings in 1995), it is common practice to supplement this with income from other employment. There is a weak relationship between contributions and benefits, which provides little incentive to contribute to the state scheme. Weak compliance and ineffective financial sanctions for late payment have compounded these structural weaknesses.

The weak financial position of the pension system has spilled over onto health provision, as a large part of the pension deficit has been financed by funds nominally raised for health insurance (up to 1994, when the health insurance system yielded a deficit as well). Spending on health care amounted to only 4 per cent of GDP in 1994, of which around two-thirds was public expenditure.[1] Only 64.2 per cent of the population was covered by health insurance schemes in 1994.

Sharply widening deficits have moved social security reform up the political agenda. Public debate of the options for reform is being encouraged by circulation of the studies made for the Turkish government by the International Labour Office and the Australian Health Insurance Commission.[2] The most pressing need is to put the pension system on to a sound actuarial basis, through substantial increases in retirement age and the insurable earnings limit on pension contributions.

The report on health concluded that better value for money could also be obtained from the public health system. Presently, health services are provided at below cost. This benefits the rich (who are more likely to be insured and who tend to use medical services more). The report recommends that subsidies should be limited to dependent children and to low-income families to target those most in need. Drawing on the experience of other OECD countries (*e.g.* the United Kingdom and New Zealand) a separation between health providers and purchasers could result in more competitive delivery of service.

---

1. See Chapter III of the *Seventh Five-Year Development Plan,* Ankara, 1996.
2. "Social Security", The International Labour Office, Geneva, and "Reform of health financing, pension and social assistance systems in Turkey", Joint Report, Australian Health Insurance Commission and International Labour Office, March 1996.

culminating a process which started in the Ankara Agreement of 1963. As of 1 January 1996, Turkey had taken or agreed to take action to:

- eliminate all customs duties and quantitative restrictions on trade in industrial commodities with the EU on 1 January 1996;
- introduce the common EU customs tariff rates against third countries and adopt all preferential agreements the EU has concluded with third countries by the year 2001;
- ensure adequate and effective protection and enforcement of intellectual, industrial and commercial property rights;[65]
- adopt the EU competition rules, including measures regarding public aid, within two years (although aid given for structural adjustment purposes will be permitted for another five years);

EU customs union will also require harmonisation of Turkish laws and procedures in related areas including quantitative restrictions, anti-dumping rules, rules of origin, patents and licenses, etc.[66] The agreement notably excludes trade in agriculture, which is under active negotiations,[67] as well as trade in services, government procurement and the movement of capital and labour.

Turkey was one of the first of the developing countries to adopt unilateral trade liberalisation in the 1980s. In December 1983 nominal (trade-weighted) tariffs were cut unilaterally from nearly 40 to 22 per cent. This impetus was followed by progressive tariff reductions in the run-up to EU customs union. By 1994, (import weighted) nominal protection rates (NPRs) with the EU had dropped to 10.2 per cent, and will drop to some 1.3 per cent once the customs union is fully in place.[68] (Comparable NPRs with third countries are 22.1 and 6.9 per cent.)

NPRs are only one element of trade protection. Turkey has no import quotas or variable levies, but the Mass Housing Fund levy (applying to over 13 000 tariff lines) averaged almost 17 per cent in 1993 and was phased out in 1995. The economy wide effective rate of protection (EPRs) is estimated to drop from some 18.4 per cent in 1994 to 1 per cent in the year 2001,[69] with much of the adjustment taking place in the first two to three years. Although the overall level of protection will be considerably lower, a wide degree of dispersion in NPRs and EPRs[70] will nonetheless remain; and this may result in continuing distortions in resource allocation.

Customs union with the EU is potentially the biggest positive supply side shock to hit the economy since the early 1980s. The effects of trade liberalisation are likely to come from:

- more efficient use of resources along the lines of comparative advantage;
- economies of scale, as international specialisation is further extended;
- real income gains for consumers as trade barriers are reduced.

The benefits of freer trade are uncontroversial. One important and comparatively robust empirical finding is that trade liberalisation has had a significant positive impact on post-war productivity growth, especially in Asia.[71] At the same time, applied general equilibrium model (AGE) estimates of the benefits of trade liberalisation (*e.g.* the Canada-US Free-Trade Agreement, Mexico's entry into NAFTA) typically show significant, albeit small one-time welfare gains of the order of 1 per cent of GDP.[72] These small gains are unsurprising, as they largely measure the deadweight burden of ''tariff wedges''. Indeed, the main economic benefits from trade probably come from the dynamic effects of scale economies, foreign direct investment inflows and heightened competition. On plausible assumptions these factors could treble estimated benefits.

AGE model estimates for the Turkish EU customs union are rare and their reliability may be limited by the quality of available data (which significantly under-represents the size of the hidden economy and its supply-side flexibility). Further, such results are sensitive to assumptions concerning how the some $2.5 billion in tariff revenue collected in 1994 will eventually be replaced. The World Bank is among the few agencies to have made AGE estimate of the Turkey-EU customs union effects. Its estimates are for static gains of some 1 per cent on the level of GDP.[73] Hence, ensuring that the Turkish economy also reaps the larger, dynamic benefits of trade liberalisation is a major policy challenge.

Although the economy as a whole will unambiguously gain from freer trade, some sectors currently sheltered by high EPRs will be faced with severe world competition and significant short-run adjustment costs (although these should be limited by the fact that industry has had over a decade to adjust). One area where Turkey will eventually face more severe competition will be in the textiles and clothing industry.[74] In addition, a number of sectors will be faced with large reductions in EPRs, notably: petroleum refining (–177 per cent), footwear

(–52 per cent), motor vehicles (–44 per cent), non-metallic mineral products (–25 per cent), glass and glass products (–24 per cent), paper and paper products (–19 per cent) and leather and fur products (–10 per cent).[75]

The EPRs cited above are at a two-digit level of industry classification. Based on the experience of other regional trade agreements, important subsets of firms or specialised industries will adapt through greater intra-industry specialisation and dynamic scale economies. The business sector is seeing the challenge of EU customs union with a certain degree of optimism.[76] Turkish industry requested no specific derogations from these tariff cuts and demonstrated an impressive ability to ''bounce back'' from the severe 1994 recession.

To sum up, the government's structural agenda has made slow and patchy progress over the past decade. Customs union with the EU provides a window of opportunity to modernise Turkey's legal framework and to transform its human and physical resource base into one able to support a modern, dynamic and more market-oriented economy. But much faster structural reform than hitherto will be necessary in areas such as tax administration, social security and privatisation, to reap the benefits from the customs union arrangements.

IV. Implementing the OECD's Jobs Strategy

Introduction

A relatively large part of non-agricultural employment in Turkey is in the informal economy. Agricultural employment is also dominated by informal arrangements, such as self-employment and unpaid family labour. Almost by definition, these sectors face a low tax wedge on wages and are largely free from most types of labour market regulation. Because of the absence of regulatory restrictions, most of the Turkish labour market can be assumed to be "flexible" in the sense that wages are free to equilibrate demand and supply in the various labour market segments. In addition, there is no unemployment insurance in Turkey[77] and other types of income assistance are quite low, so work incentives are not significantly altered by government transfer systems. In some sense, then, it is disconcerting to note that measured unemployment is fairly high in Turkey, especially in urban areas where the unemployment rate was about 12 per cent in 1994. For the economy as a whole the average unemployment and "underemployment" rates[78] were both 8.2 per cent in 1994. The unemployment rate has been largely stable since 1970 except for a bulge in the late 1970s (Figure 18). The incidence of long term unemployment – with 44 per cent of unemployed being without a job for one year or more – is among the highest in the OECD area (OECD, 1996*a*). However, caution should be used in comparing the Turkish labour force survey with those of other Member countries because Turkish survey methodology increases the measured unemployment rate relative to most other countries' survey methods (see Box 3). The period since 1970 has also witnessed a secular decline in the employment rate (Figure 18).

At a very fundamental level, though, labour market problems in Turkey go beyond the measured rate of open unemployment. These problems can be summarised by a simple and obvious notion: that a significant portion of the popula-

Box 3. **The labour force survey in Turkey**

Prior to 1988, several institutions gathered data on the Turkish labour force. The Turkish State Institute of Statistics (SIS), for example, launched its first household labour force survey in 1966. Between then and 1988, several other surveys were performed by various organisations at irregular intervals. This led to a series of surveys varying in methodology, definitions and areas covered. A new household labour force survey procedure was introduced by the SIS in 1988 and it has since been performed twice a year (in April and October). The survey questionnaire is designed to conform as closely as possible to international data gathering norms, but some potentially important differences remain.

The main difference involves the length of the search period that is used (among other criteria) to determine whether someone without a job is unemployed or inactive. The data convention underlying most OECD countries' surveys considers a person to be unemployed if that person is without a job in the reference week and has been looking for a job in the past four weeks. In Turkey, however, a search period of 6 months is used. If the one-month definition were used, a portion of Turkey's measured unemployment would shift into the inactive category. It is impossible to say how large this effect might be. A second difference with most other countries' labour force surveys is that, in Turkey, the minimum age for the working age population is 12 years, whereas, elsewhere, this minimum age is usually 15 (in some countries 14 or 16). The OECD data reported in this chapter removes the 12-14 age cohort from the Turkish data in order to make it comparable with other member countries' data.

The survey sample is designed to be representative of households in Turkey with respect to regions, rural-urban residence and other socio-economic variables. The survey also seeks to capture the various forms of employment whose incidence is high in Turkey (*e.g.* informal paid employment, self-employment, unpaid family work). The sample size is small, however, in relation to Turkey's population of 60 million people. The sample for the Turkish labour force survey of April 1994 consisted of 11 160 households, which is much smaller relative to population than the sample sizes of other Member countries. For example, the Netherlands had a labour force survey sample of 117 000 households in 1994 (compared with a population of 15 million), the Canadian sample in November 1995 was 52 000 households (population 29 million) and in Sweden the 1995 sample size was 216 000 persons (population 5.5 million). This means that, while the data for Turkey as a whole may be quite reliable, the labour force statistics based on sample sub-sets (for example, unemployment rates by age cohort, region or sex) could have high variances due to their relatively small sample sizes.

tion lives in moderate to extreme poverty. About 60-70 per cent of Turkey's population lives in rural areas or in squatter settlements (Bulutay, 1995). Many of these people work in low-productivity jobs at correspondingly low wages.

Figure 18. **LABOUR MARKET INDICATORS**

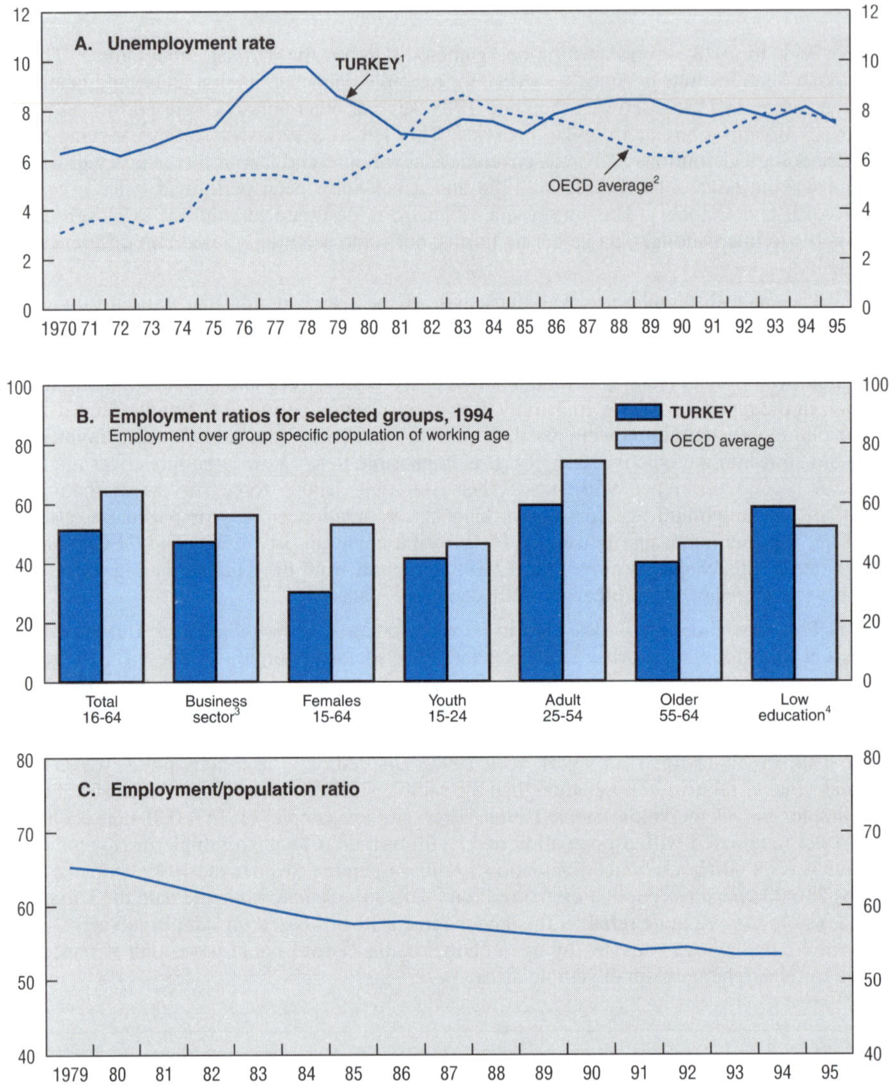

1. Data for 1995 are OECD estimates.
2. OECD standardised unemployment rates for 18 countries, excluding Mexico, Austria, Denmark, Iceland, Greece, Luxembourg and Turkey.
3. Business sector employment divided by working age population.
4. Individuals aged 25-64 years who have not completed upper secondary school.

Source: OECD, *Labour Force Statistics, Main Economic Indicators* and *Education at a Glance.*

Employment is frequently precarious and often does not allow workers to build up human capital. In this respect, Turkey's labour market problems are related more closely to those of the ''working poor'' than to the ''poverty of exclusion''. Turkey does not have a large mass of unemployed who, because of restrictive labour market policies, are unable to bid themselves into a job. However, family transfers permit large numbers of people to engage in job search or to remain inactive. Nevertheless, because the public social safety net in Turkey is still rudimentary, workers face strong incentives to generate some sort of income and they are often very resourceful in doing this. Thus, aside from some reforms needed in parts of the formal sector, the labour market challenges facing Turkey are somewhat different from those facing many other member countries. Turkey's challenge will be to reinforce the existing strengths of its labour markets and to speed up building the institutional foundations of a more advanced economy so as to promote a sustainable increase in living standards for the bulk of its population.

This chapter follows up the general structural policy recommendations of the OECD Jobs Study with specific recommendations for Turkey. The structure of the chapter is as follows. The first section contains an overview of the Turkish labour market and employment performance over the past two decades. The policy requirements for Turkey emerging from the Jobs Study are discussed in the second part, while a review of recent policy actions and an assessment of the scope for further action are given in the last section.

Labour market and employment performance

Labour market developments over the last several decades have reflected the two dominant trends in Turkey's post-war economy. First, the high rate of population growth has translated into correspondingly high growth of the working age population. Population growth, although slowing down recently, has averaged about 2.5 per cent per year since 1950, while annual employment growth for the economy as whole has averaged 1.8 per cent over the same period. Emigration also absorbed large numbers of people, though the pace of emigration has slowed somewhat in recent years.[79] Second, rural-urban migration and the associated shift in jobs from agriculture to industry and services have progressed rapidly, although agriculture's employment share remains high (45 per cent in

1994, as compared with 6 per cent in 1994 in the OECD area generally).[80] Non-agricultural employment grew at a 4.7 per cent annual pace over the 1950-90 period. Thus, most of the post war period was characterised by strong non-agricultural (and mainly urban) job growth. In recent years, though, employment growth has slackened and, during the 1990s, net job creation in urban areas has been well under urban population growth (Erocal, 1995). This has meant that the long-term decline in agriculture's share of total employment has been reversed and it has inched up again in some recent years (Figure 19).

These developments have been accompanied by two related labour market phenomena – relatively high unemployment and low participation rates in urban areas. As observed in many other OECD countries, the incidence of unemployment is unevenly distributed across the various socio-economic groups. For example, the incidence is much higher among young people and urban women (Table 12). Turkey follows the general OECD pattern in that its youth unemploy-

Figure 19. **SECTORAL COMPOSITION OF TOTAL EMPLOYMENT**

As a percentage of working age population

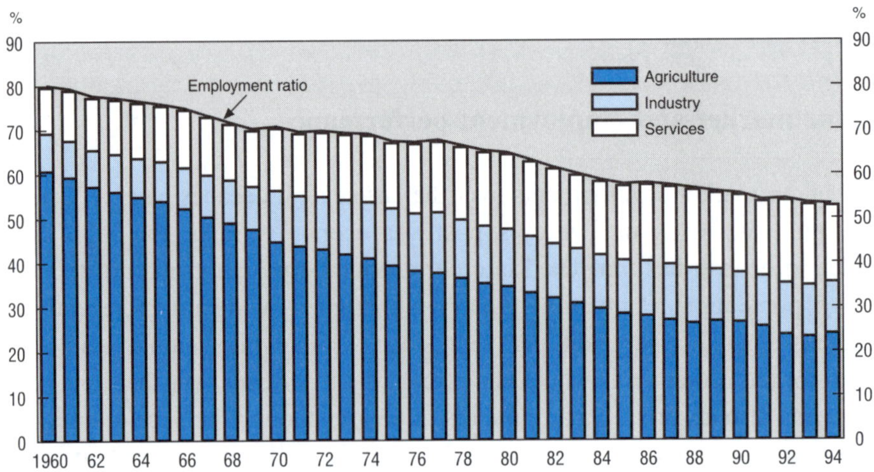

Source: OECD, *Labour Force Statistics.*

Table 12. **Unemployment rate by age and sex**

Per cent of labour force in corresponding age and sex group

	Males				Females			
	Total	15-24	25-54	55-64	Total	15-24	25-54	55-64
	1983							
United States	9.9	18.4	8.2	6.1	9.2	15.8	7.7	5.0
Japan	2.7	4.6	2.0	5.0	2.6	4.5	2.4	2.1
Germany	7.3	10.4	6.3	9.0	8.8	11.7	8.0	8.6
Portugal	4.7	13.2	2.6	1.9	11.6	24.6	8.6	2.2
Spain	15.6	33.7	11.5	8.8	20.5	43.7	11.6	2.9
Turkey	**7.9**	**16.7**	**5.4**	**3.7**	**7.7**	**13.1**	**5.5**	**0.5**
OECD average	7.9	16.5	6.1	5.7	10.1	19.4	7.4	4.8
	1990							
United States	5.6	11.6	4.5	3.8	5.4	10.6	4.5	2.8
Japan	2.0	4.5	1.4	3.4	2.2	4.1	2.1	1.4
Germany	5.4	5.3	4.7	9.9	7.4	6.0	7.1	15.2
Portugal	3.1	7.8	2.1	2.2	6.5	13.1	5.5	1.8
Spain	12.0	26.2	9.3	8.4	24.2	39.7	20.6	7.2
Turkey	**8.0**	**16.6**	**5.2**	**3.9**	**8.7**	**15.0**	**5.9**	**1.7**
OECD average	6.0	12.0	4.9	4.6	8.6	14.8	7.4	4.5
	1994							
United States	6.2	13.2	4.9	4.4	6.0	11.6	5.0	3.9
Japan	2.8	5.6	2.0	4.5	3.0	5.3	2.8	1.9
Germany	7.6	8.1	6.9	12.6	10.4	8.3	10.3	17.3
Portugal	4.5	9.8	3.5	4.1	6.5	14.9	5.4	2.2
Spain	19.5	37.4	16.4	13.3	31.4	50.1	28.4	9.8
Turkey	**8.6**	**17.3**	**6.1**	**2.9**	**7.8**	**13.0**	**5.7**	**0.5**
OECD average	8.9	17.7	7.6	7.3	10.5	18.9	9.2	6.2

Source: OECD, *Labour Force Statistics, Part III,* 1995, except for Turkey which comes from OECD, *Economies at a Glance: Structural Indicators,* 1996.

ment rate is consistently about twice the total unemployment rate. Unemployment, as typically measured, is also a predominantly urban phenomenon[81] (Table 13).

In the OECD as a whole, unemployment rates tend to be inversely related to the level of educational attainment. In Turkey, the relationship between unemployment rates and education is unusual in that rates are higher among workers with mid-level qualifications (lower secondary and secondary diplomas). Workers with either very low qualifications (primary school or less) or with very high

Table 13. **The socio-economic dimensions of unemployment**

As a per cent of the labour force in age group

	Urban			Rural			All Turkey		
	Total	*of which:*		Total	*of which:*		Total	*of which:*	
		First time job seekers	Other		First time job seekers	Other		First time job seekers	Others
Female									
Aged 15+	19.6	12.0	7.6	1.9	1.3	0.6	6.8	4.2	2.6
Aged 15-24	28.3	18.6	9.7	4.2	3.2	1.0	11.5	7.9	3.6
Aged 25+	14.6	8.3	6.4	0.9	0.4	0.5	4.5	2.4	2.0
Male									
Aged 15+	11.2	3.4	7.9	6.4	2.2	4.2	9.0	2.8	6.2
Aged 15-24	23.8	13.2	10.7	13.2	7.6	5.6	18.6	10.4	8.2
Aged 25+	7.9	0.7	7.1	4.3	0.5	3.8	6.3	0.6	5.6
Both sexes									
Aged 15+	12.8	4.9	7.8	2.8	1.8	2.8	8.4	3.3	5.1
Aged 15-24	25.1	14.7	10.4	3.4	5.5	3.4	15.8	9.4	6.4
Aged 25+	8.9	1.9	7.0	3.0	0.4	2.6	5.8	1.1	4.7

Source: State Institute of Statistics, *Household Labour Force Survey*, April 1994.

qualifications (university diplomas) tend to have lower unemployment rates (Table 14). This pattern is particularly pronounced among women. The unemployment rate for women with mid-level qualifications was well over two and one half times the rates for women having only primary education and for those having longer university qualifications. These patterns of unemployment can be attributed to the operation of family transfer systems, which are described in the section on wage formation.

Participation rates for men in Turkey are about average for the OECD, but declined from 83.7 per cent in 1983 to 80.8 per cent in 1994. Most of the decline occurred in the 55-64 year age group (Table 15). Similar declines for males, especially for older males, have been observed in other OECD countries. For male youth, the participation rate is much higher than the OECD average, due mainly to the low school enrolment rate for this group (see below). Participation rates for the other male age cohorts are about average. The female participation rate is very low by OECD standards (33.6 per cent in 1994, as compared with an OECD average of 59.1 per cent (OECD, 1996*a*). The female participation rate

Table 14. **Unemployment rate by level of educational attainment, 1991**

Level of education [1]		20-24	25-29	30-34	35-44	45-54	55-64	25-64
					Males			
All		21.0	9.5	4.0	4.0	4.5	4.9	5.4
Early childhood and primary	0, 1	16.4	8.4	4.7	4.6	4.5	3.8	5.3
Basic	2	26.1	13.8	4.2	6.0	6.5	6.1	8.6
Upper secondary	3	28.0	10.3	2.8	1.0	5.9	22.4	5.6
Shorter tertiary	5	0.0	0.0	0.0	0.0	0.0	0.0	0.0
Longer tertiary	6, 7	36.7	6.2	1.3	1.0	1.7	6.0	2.3
					Females			
All		15.4	11.0	8.6	4.3	1.4	2.4	6.8
Early childhood and primary	0, 1	5.6	6.3	8.0	4.9	0.8	1.3	5.1
Basic	2	25.1	15.9	22.4	6.0	0.0	0.0	14.6
Upper secondary	3	39.7	22.6	8.8	4.9	11.3	50.1	14.2
Shorter tertiary	5	0.0	0.0	0.0	0.0	0.0	0.0	0.0
Longer tertiary	6, 7	38.6	14.8	4.6	0.0	7.3	0.0	5.8

1. The numbers in the second column correspond to the level of education as defined in the International Standard Classification of Education (ISCED).

Source: OECD Jobs Study, 1994.

Table 15. **Participation rates by age and sex**

Per cent of population in corresponding age and sex group

	Males				Females			
	Total	15-24	25-54	55-64	Total	15-24	25-54	55-64
	1983							
United States	87.6	72.5	93.8	69.4	63.5	61.9	67.1	41.5
Japan	89.0	43.9	97.1	84.7	57.2	44.4	59.5	46.1
Germany	82.6	61.0	94.3	63.1	52.5	54.8	58.3	26.3
Portugal	88.7	70.7	94.5	70.4	61.1	63.9	64.3	33.7
Spain	85.0	68.3	94.5	71.5	34.7	46.1	33.3	20.3
Turkey	**83.7**	**70.0**	**94.9**	**62.0**	**35.2**	**38.8**	**34.9**	**26.7**
OECD average	84.2	61.4	94.5	64.0	53.1	52.4	57.4	30.6
	1990							
United States	88.3	71.5	93.5	67.7	69.8	63.1	74.1	45.3
Japan	88.1	43.4	97.5	83.3	60.4	44.8	64.2	47.2
Germany	80.8	62.0	91.2	57.7	57.0	57.4	64.1	26.4
Portugal	84.3	61.1	94.0	66.9	59.7	52.7	68.0	32.5
Spain	79.3	54.6	94.1	62.4	42.2	47.5	46.9	19.5
Turkey	**83.6**	**71.8**	**94.2**	**61.2**	**36.0**	**39.4**	**36.0**	**26.6**
OECD average	82.7	60.0	93.6	59.3	58.4	53.4	65.2	31.3
	1994							
United States	87.0	70.3	91.7	65.5	71.4	62.5	75.3	48.9
Japan	90.6	48.0	97.5	85.0	62.1	47.1	65.3	48.1
Germany	78.0	58.5	89.2	51.5	60.8	55.2	71.0	26.8
Portugal	81.9	53.1	93.9	62.5	60.6	43.2	72.3	32.8
Spain	78.0	54.7	92.9	56.1	45.8	43.1	54.3	19.3
Turkey	**80.8**	**64.7**	**93.4**	**58.9**	**33.6**	**36.1**	**33.8**	**25.0**
OECD average	81.0	55.9	92.3	56.8	59.1	49.0	67.2	32.1

Source: OECD, *Labour Force Statistics, Part III,* 1995, except for Turkey which comes from State Institute of Statistics, *Household Labour Force Survey,* April 1994 and October 1994.

has been declining for years, due mainly to rural-urban migration and partly to the increase in schooling rates. The female participation rate in rural areas is high because women often work as unpaid family labourers on farms. In urban labour markets, though, their participation rate is quite low (16.2 per cent in October 1994). Thus, migration from rural to urban areas tends to lower the overall female participation rate as well as the measured employment rate.

Policy requirements

The employment generating capacity of the economy has historically been strong. In recent years, though, the rate and types of job creation have not been sufficient to meet the formidable challenges facing Turkey. The following section argues that Turkey's largely flexible labour markets mean that the problems facing Turkey do not centre exclusively on unemployment, but also on the "low quality" of many jobs currently available in the economy. However, these jobs match the skills and education attainment of large parts of the Turkish workforce. Thus, in some sense, the roots of the problem lie in the low level of human capital accumulation and the lack of suitable institutions to promote such capital accumulation. This points to a need for additional efforts to accumulate human and institutional capital to facilitate Turkey's transition to a more advanced stage of development. The term "institutional capital" refers to the set of organisations, laws and business practices that are required to sustain an advanced economy. These include the legal and information infrastructure needed by formal labour markets; a diverse array of financial institutions (for example, specialising in meeting the needs of start-up companies or of small businesses); research and development infrastructure; formal contract enforcement and an effective judicial service; and advanced structures for human capital accumulation (such as a dense network of schools, a diverse array of universities and other institutes of tertiary education, curricula and standards for teaching at all levels, skills certification procedures, etc.). The further development of many of these institutions in Turkey will require judicious assistance from the public sector. Yet, Turkey has not so far been able to initiate a comprehensive process of public sector reform.

The deficiencies in public sector management stem from the poor focus of government activities: the government is heavily involved in areas where it has little "organisational comparative advantage" and is insufficiently committed in other areas where it has a vital role to play. Thus, as discussed in this chapter and in Chapter III, Turkey runs large public deficits and, yet, has problems in the provision of some basic public services. Far from responding sufficiently to the needs of broad swathes of the Turkish population over the last several decades, the political process in Turkey has often been dominated by political constituencies and by vested business interests. As in many other member countries, these groups have captured Turkey's political process and have deflected government programmes and expenditures to their own benefit (Atiyas, 1995). To a significant extent, they have also succeeded in shifting the financing of these expenditures onto the general public (through taxation, public debt and inflation). From time to time (*e.g.* during the late 1970s and in 1994) the financial imbalances inherent in this political process have reached crisis proportions. These crises have provided windows of opportunity for implementing major reform programmes. Today – crisis or not – Turkey's main policy challenges hinge on thorough public sector reform.

Enhancing the ability to adjust and adapt

Wage formation process

Labour markets in Turkey encompass a range of wage setting mechanisms. First, there are agricultural labour markets where earnings are dominated by the returns to self-employment and to unpaid family labour. In the non-agricultural economy, wage setting mechanisms vary with the different labour market segments: informal employment; plus self-employment; formal public employment; and formal private employment. Rough estimates of the numbers of people employed in these segments are provided in Box 4. The Box gives estimates indicating that the large majority of workers – about 66 per cent in 1993 – work in agriculture or in the informal non-agricultural sector. Few studies of wage formation in the informal sector are available. Wages can, however, be assumed to be responsive to changing macroeconomic, sectoral or local conditions. Publicly-sponsored social assistance schemes do not provide high enough benefits to constitute a serious disincentive to work. However, transfer systems internal to the family provide the resources for certain parts of the urban labour force to remain unemployed (especially for young people) or not to participate in labour markets (especially for urban women).

The family's willingness to finance unemployment or non-participation is important for labour market clearing in Turkey (judging from the high unemployment rates and low participation rates observed for some socio-economic groups). This willingness is presumably influenced by the wages and the working conditions that the family member can command in the labour market, by the value of unpaid family services that the person can provide, by the value of leisure and by

Box 4. **Formal and informal employment**

This Box provides estimates of the number of workers employed in various parts of the formal and informal economy in Turkey. The line dividing the formal and informal economy is indistinct and much depends on the definition used. For example, one feature of much of the Turkish labour market is the informality of job search and information dissemination processes. Job search and hiring procedures tend to by-pass formal information and search systems such as job banks, employment services or advertising. Likewise, informal labour markets tend to make little use of the more sophisticated labour contracting that is often observed in more advanced economic activities. In much of Turkey's labour market, the development of many of these institutions is rudimentary. Thus, for example, people are likely to apply for jobs with and to hire people who are family members or who come from the same village. Indeed, in the absence of formal contracting in the workplace, there are undoubtedly good reasons for this reliance on close family or village ties. These presumably provide alternative ways of establishing and enforcing work-related agreements. Another characteristic of informal enterprises is that they tend to operate outside the controls and obligations imposed by labour force regulation, tax rules and other legal constraints on firm behaviour. Here, again, the distinction between formal and informal firms is probably a matter of degree, with compliance being almost non-existent in the informal sector and relatively strict (but not perfect) in the formal sector.

Thus, the border separating the formal and informal economies is necessarily indistinct. Generally, the formal economy relies heavily on the labour market institutions that are commonly associated with more advanced economies – formal job search and hiring, more elaborate contracting between employees and firms, greater adherence to societal obligations on firms through regulation or taxation. In contrast, the informal economy relies relatively little on these institutions.

Agricultural employment – 45 per cent of total employment in 1994 – mainly comprises the self-employed and unpaid family workers. In general, the organisation of agricultural labour relations is informal. Turkey's non-agricultural labour market is difficult to classify. It is dominated by two types of employment: 1) employment in the public sector (which is always formal); 2) employment in the private sector, which may or may not be formal. Estimates of employment in these categories are provided below:

- **Employment in the public sector.** The government's share of total employment in 1993 was about 13 per cent if state economic enterprises (SEEs) are included, and 9.8 per cent if they are not included. The comparable figure for an unweighted average of 24 OECD countries (OECD, 1996) in 1993 was 17.9 per cent, excluding SEE-type institutions. The public share of wage employment is about one third, which is similar to the shares observed in Scandinavian countries – the highest in the OECD area. Thus, while public employment is not high relative to total employment, it accounts for a large share of wage earners.
- **Employment in the private non-agricultural sector.** Using Ministry of Labour registrations for 1993, one can estimate the number of informal wage

(continued on next page)

(continued)

earners by subtracting the number of registered wage earners from the total number of wage earners given in the Labour Force Survey. This estimate shows Turkey as having 2.3 million informal wage earners in the private sector. The number of non-agricultural unpaid family workers was 468 000 in 1993. Roughly half of non-agricultural self-employment – about 800 000 – can be assumed to be in the informal sector. This estimate also includes the roughly 600 000 employers with fewer than 4 employees in the informal sector. Adding up the components, one finds that some 4.1 million workers (or 21 per cent of total employment) were in the informal non-agricultural sector in 1993 (Figure 20).

Figure 20. **LABOUR MARKET SEGMENTS IN TURKEY,[1] 1993**

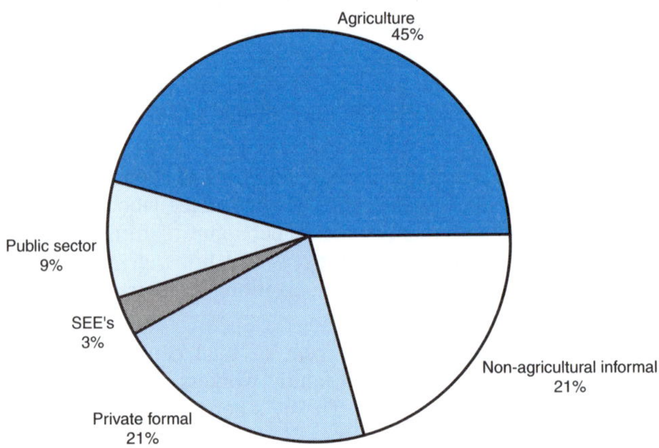

1. Employment shares by sector; estimates from Household Labour Force Surveys and Erocal (1995).
Source: OECD.

the economic status of the family. Many families in Turkey are not so poor that they are willing to oblige all family members to work, regardless of the wage and type of work.[82] Thus, institutional arrangements in the informal economy are such that wages settle at a market clearing level, adjusted for families' willingness to bid significant numbers of people out of work at prevailing wages. For many workers with low skills, the market wage can be very low indeed.

Wage setting in the formal sector is governed by quite different institutional arrangements. As discussed in Box 4, the formal sector – consisting of the civil service, employment in State Economic Enterprises (SEEs), and private formal employment – accounts for only about 27 per cent of total employment. Civil service wages are set by government. Civil servants have only recently been allowed to form unions and are not allowed to strike. The government determines wages and civil service employment on the basis of political and budgetary factors. SEE workers tend to be heavily unionised (they accounted for about 63 per cent of the workers covered by collective agreements between 1989 and 1994).[83] There is also a small unionised segment in the private enterprise sector.[84] Negotiations for both SEE and private workers' collective agreements set wages for a two year period. The agreements deal with Turkey's high inflation rate by specifying in advance a series of step-wise increases in salaries, with the increases generally occurring every six months (there is no indexing).[85] The minimum wage is determined every year by the Minimum Wage Setting Commission, which consists of the government, and employer and worker representatives.[86]

These arrangements have led to the following trends in formal sector wages:

– Civil service labour costs and net salaries have grown quickly over the 1988-93 period. Figure 21 plots the number of civil servants and net salaries and labour costs per civil servant in constant 1987 Turkish lira from 1987 to 1994. The figure shows that, over the 1988-93 period, real net salaries began a steep upward climb while the growth in the number of civil servants accelerated to 4.4 per cent per year. This has meant that the civil service wage bill grew at an annual rate of 20.3 per cent in real terms between 1988 and 1993.[87] This development was reversed between 1993 and 1994, when the real civil service wage bill fell by 22 per cent.
– Labour costs in SEEs rose above those in the large private sector enterprises in June 1989 and have remained higher for the rest of the period (Figure 22). The figure shows that public and private wage costs in the formal manufacturing sector tracked each other quite closely over the

Figure 21. **EMPLOYMENT AND COMPENSATION IN THE CIVIL SERVICE**

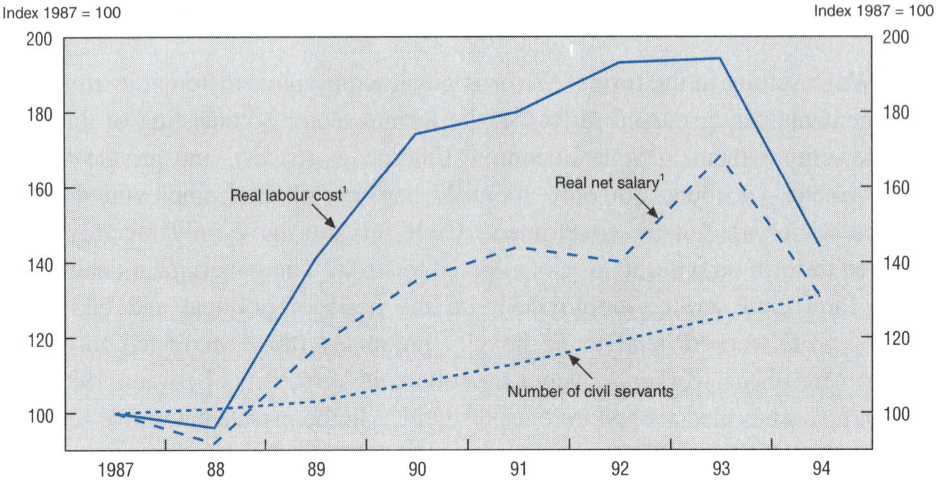

1. Deflated by the urban consumer price index.
Source: State Planning Organisation.

1988-94 period. The recent sharp drop in both sectors' wage and non-wage labour costs reflects the austerity programme undertaken by the government in 1994.

Since little is known about wage formation in the informal sector, the relationship between informal and formal wage setting cannot be examined rigorously. It seems clear, though, that many workers view employment in the public sector as an attractive prospect. This is supported (indirectly) by data on labour turnover among registered workers in the public and private enterprise sectors. These data show job turnover for registered workers (by reason for separation) for seven half-year periods between 1992 and 1995 (see Table 16). Dismissals and "other" reasons for separation were somewhat lower in public enterprises than in private ones.[88] The difference in the number of voluntary separations (quits) was striking, though. Among SEE workers the half-year quit rate (over the 1992-95 period) was only 0.2 per cent, as compared with 8.3 per cent among the private firms' employees. Generally, then, one can infer that the public enterprise sector offers an attractive package of job security, work effort,

Figure 22. **WAGE AND NON-WAGE COSTS IN LARGE MANUFACTURING ENTERPRISES**

Per month, 1987 prices

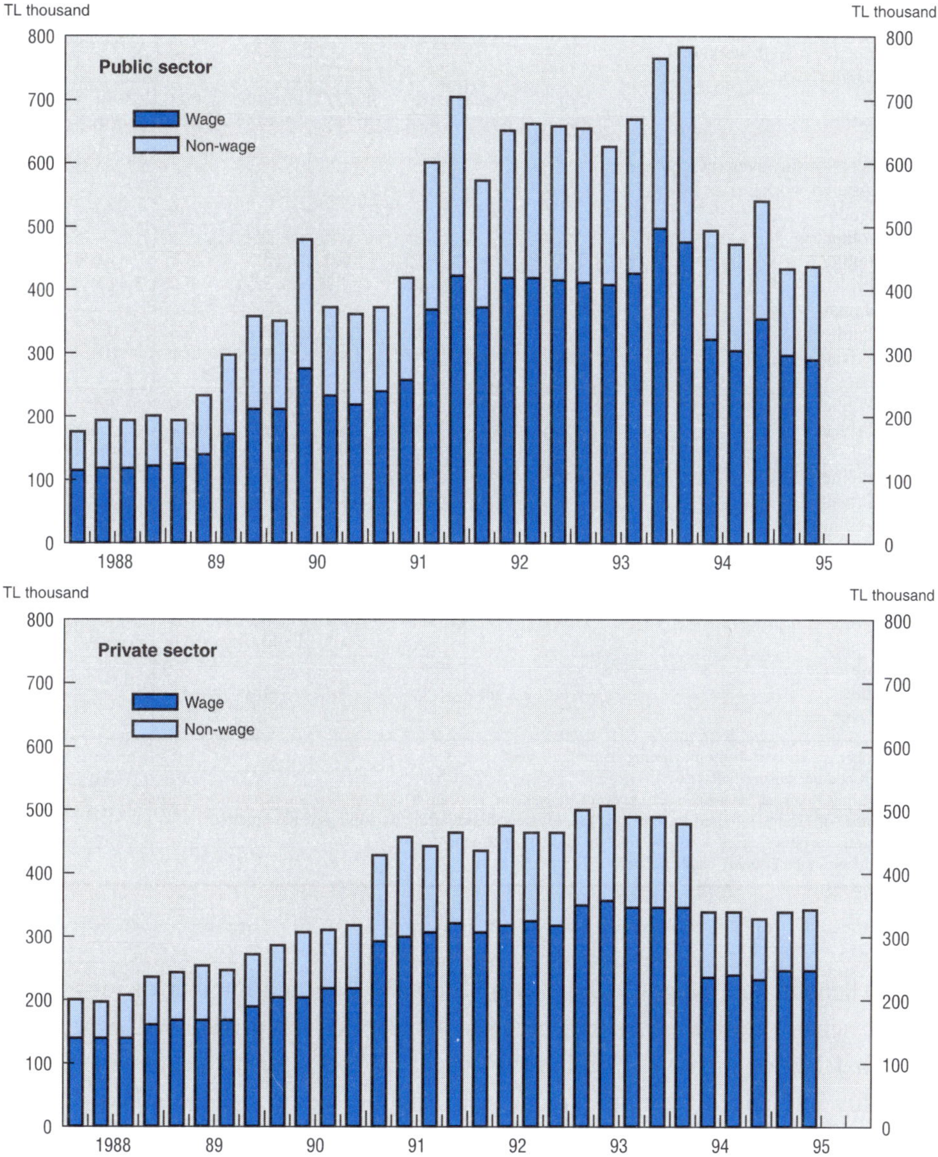

Source: State Institute of Statistics, *Quarterly Manufacturing Surveys Results.*

Table 16. **Turnover of registered workers**

	1992		1993		1994		1995	Period average
	I	II	I	II	I	II	I	
Number of registered workers[1] (thousands)								
Public	970	965	1 019	1 027	1 045	1 003	994	
Private	2 636	2 631	2 664	2 715	2 793	2 813	2 840	
Components of turnover (percentage of registered workers)								
Separations								
Involuntary[2]								
Public	2.6	1.1	2.5	1.0	3.5	3.2	1.6	2.2
Private	3.2	2.7	2.6	2.2	3.6	3.2	1.9	2.8
Voluntary[2]								
Public	0.2	0.2	0.2	0.2	0.3	0.3	0.2	0.2
Private	9.4	9.2	7.7	8.2	9.0	8.1	6.6	8.3
Other[2, 3]								
Public	3.2	2.6	3.7	2.0	3.5	4.0	1.8	3.0
Private	4.8	4.7	5.0	5.2	7.0	6.2	5.3	5.5
Total[2]								
Public	6.0	4.0	6.3	3.2	7.3	7.5	3.6	5.4
Private	17.4	16.6	15.3	15.7	19.6	17.5	13.9	16.6
Implied hirings[4]								
Public	5.6	9.6	7.1	4.9	3.3	6.6		6.2
Private	17.2	17.9	17.2	18.5	20.3	18.5		18.3
Gross job turnover[5]								
Public	11.6	13.6	13.4	8.1	10.6	14.1		11.9
Private	34.5	34.5	32.5	34.2	40.0	36.0		35.3
Net job creation								
Public	–0.5	5.6	0.7	1.7	–4.0	–0.8		0.5
Private	–0.2	1.2	1.9	2.9	–0.7	1.0		1.3

1. Number of workers at the beginning of the half-year.
2. Total number during half-year.
3. Including ''natural'' reasons such as death, retirement, relocation, and termination of temporary work.
4. Number of hirings required to reach the employment figure at the beginning of next period.
5. Separations plus hirings as a percentage of initial employment.

Source: Ministry of Labour, cited in Erocal 1995.

social benefits and wages.[89] Since there are only a certain number of jobs in the public sector, most workers are forced to ''make do'' on private and, especially, informal labour markets. Equilibrium wages in the informal sector are almost certainly influenced by employment in the public sector, but the relationship is complex.[90]

In conclusion, given the current relative sizes of the formal and informal sectors, the scope for reform designed to enhance wage flexibility appears to be fairly limited in Turkey. Much of the economy operates outside the influence of labour market regulation and collective bargaining. Even in the formal sector, the principal problem with wage formation is not due primarily to wage rigidities. Rather the problems reside more in the fact that formal labour markets are heavily influenced by an employer – the Turkish government – that does not face a binding budget constraint. One symptom of this has been the extremely rapid growth of the civil service wage bill over the last decade. Thus, the government has absorbed significant portions of formal sector employment growth, raising concerns as to whether these human resources have been deployed in ways that were efficient and welfare enhancing for Turkish society. The imposition of a binding budget constraint on the government would not only free up resources that could then be directed at much needed improvements in such areas as education and health, but would also promote the formation of wages that provide better signals for deploying formal sector labour across occupations and sectors.

Increasing the flexibility of employment and working time

In the informal sector, employment conditions are presumably very flexible. More precisely, if there are constraints in informal labour markets, they are ones that private agents have built in, not ones mandated by labour market regulation.[91] In the public and private parts of the formal sector, however, some labour market regulations have effects that are similar to employment protection measures. The most important of these is severance payments, which are based both on regulation and collective agreement. These can act as a significant deterrent to dismissals (especially collective dismissals) because they mean that a firm must suddenly pay off its severance liabilities if it wishes to reduce its workforce. Because severance payments tend to rise steeply after 5 years of tenure, the payments also raise the cost of dismissing longer-tenure workers. In principle, these measures apply equally to the private and public parts of the formal sector. In practice, though, they are not equally binding on all formal sector firms. For example, before workers reach tenures at which severance pay begins to rise steeply, there is a tendency in the private sector to dismiss workers (or to induce them to quit) and then to re-hire them.

Severance pay was originally mandated as a substitute for unemployment insurance. It also often functions as a pension premium. At present, Turkey has no unemployment insurance system, but several proposals for such a system are now circulating. The government foresees the setting up of an unemployment insurance system which provides limited compensation for a limited period. The intent is that the system will remain largely self-financing with little need for public support. While such proposals are guided by good intentions of alleviating hardship, Turkey should exercise caution in implementing such a system if the serious mistakes made in other member countries are to be avoided (see "Assessment and Scope for Further Action" below).

Turkey also has limits on collective and forced unpaid leave. These restrictions are based partly on regulation and partly on collective agreements. During the crisis of 1994, however, private sector firms frequently did make use of unpaid leave. Both the unions and the government were compelled to turn a blind eye to this infringement of regulatory and contractual rights (Erocal, 1995). A notification period of 2 to 8 weeks is required (this may be extended by collective bargaining) and wages for these weeks may be paid to dismissed workers. Thus, labour practices in parts of the formal sector appear to be fairly restrictive, especially for the SEEs that consistently implement them.

Taxes and transfers

The wedge separating total labour costs paid by employers and net earnings received by (formal sector) workers is quite high, but it decreased slightly over the 1991-94 period. Preparations for further decreases are in progress. The share of take-home pay for the "average production worker" rose from 65.2 per cent to 68.8 per cent of the gross earnings over the period. Yet the worker's share of take-home pay is still almost 4 percentage points lower than the 1994 OECD average (Table 17). In particular, the average income tax rate is high; an employee earning the income of an average production worker pays 26.1 per cent of his gross earnings as income tax, which is the fourth highest proportion in the OECD area. The tax wedge is even larger for the lower-paid workers because there is a ceiling on both employees' and employers' social security contributions. This ceiling is already reached by an employee earning one third of what an average production worker earns.

Thus, for the relatively small number of workers and firms paying taxes, the burden can be quite heavy. Some reform focusing on broadening the tax base would appear, therefore, to be desirable. The narrowness of the tax base stems

Table 17. **Income and payroll taxes, 1994**

For a single person earning the income of an average production worker

	Average rate of income tax paid	Social security contributions: Employees' contributions	Social security contributions: Employers' compulsory contributions to schemes operated within the government sector	Take home pay plus cash transfers	Tax wedge: difference between labour costs and take home pay plus cash transfers
	Per cent of gross earnings				Per cent of total labour costs
United States	18.2	7.7	7.7	74.1	31.2
Japan	8.7	7.0	7.5	84.3	21.6
Germany	18.8	19.4	19.4	61.8	48.3
France	8.8	18.6	..	72.6	..
Italy	16.7	10.0	46.1	73.3	49.9
United Kingdom	18.1	8.4	10.2	73.5	33.3
Canada	21.5	5.4	6.6	73.1	31.4
Australia	22.1	1.4	0.0	76.5	23.5
Austria	7.4	18.1	23.6	74.5	39.7
Belgium	24.2	13.1	34.8	62.7	53.5
Denmark	38.3	6.9	..	54.8	..
Finland	28.6	8.6	3.8	62.8	39.4
Iceland	20.4	0.3	2.8	79.3	22.9
Ireland	23.2	7.7	12.2	69.1	38.4
Luxembourg	12.9	12.5	15.0	74.6	35.1
Mexico	7.1	5.1	19.4	87.8	26.5
Netherlands	7.8	33.5	7.9	58.7	45.6
New Zealand	24.3	0.0	0.0	75.7	24.3
Norway	21.0	7.8	12.8	71.2	36.9
Portugal	7.2	11.0	24.5	81.8	34.3
Spain	12.9	6.6	31.6	80.5	38.8
Sweden	28.8	2.0	19.5	69.2	42.1
Switzerland	11.1	10.3	10.3	78.6	28.7
Turkey	**26.1**	**5.1**	**7.1**	**68.8**	**35.7**
OECD average[1]	18.1	9.4	14.7	72.5	35.5

1. Unweighted average of above data.

Source: OECD 1995, *The Tax/Benefit Position of Production Workers, Annual Report, 1991-94.*

Table 18. **Enrolment ratios**

Percentage, 1965-90

	Primary			Secondary		
	1965	1980	1990	1965	1980	1990
Turkey	**77**	**100**	**102**	**16**	**35**	**51**[1]
Middle East and North Africa	76	94	97	17	45	49
East Asia Pacific	88	89	127	–	48	49
Latin America, Caribbean	98	93	107	20	42	49
OECD	104	101	104	63	87.5	93

1. Enrolment rates for the first three years of secondary school in Turkey were 24 per cent in 1965, 42 per cent in 1980 and 59 per cent in 1990. Comparable figures for the next three years of secondary school were 12 per cent, 29 and 37 per cent respectively.

Source: Tansel, A. and A. Kazemi (1995), ''Equity in Educational Expenditures in the Middle East and North Africa'', manuscript, and State Planning Organisation.

primarily from the fact that businesses and workers in the informal economy do not pay most types of tax (including not only payroll and wage taxes but also taxes on earnings, real property and other taxes on businesses). This presumably constitutes one of the informal sector's main competitive advantages. Therefore, the objective of base broadening presents the authorities with a dilemma. On the one hand, stricter enforcement is needed to broaden the tax base. On the other hand, such enforcement – if successful – might impede the most dynamic part of the Turkish economy, the informal economy. For this reason, a ''carrot and stick'' approach to improved tax administration would appear to be desirable. Under this approach the ''stick'' of tighter enforcement and larger fines for non-compliance would be complemented with measures seeking to induce firms to join the formal economy. Parts of the informal sector must be hurt by these measures given the need to maintain small, low visibility business units. In addition, the informal sector does not benefit fully from certain public services such as contract enforcement (through judicial and police services).[92] If the quality of these services were sufficiently high, then firms might find it more cost-effective to pay taxes than to provide these services on their own or to do without. Significant parts of the informal economy are probably destined to remain there for the foreseeable future,[93] but some of the more sophisticated, informal sector firms might find that entry into the formal sector gives them a competitive boost. Here, again, the ''carrot'' part of a strategy for more effective

Box 5. **Social transfers in Turkey**

This Box describes some characteristics of Turkey's safety net. Social expenditure accounted for 6.0 per cent of GDP in 1994 (up from 3.6 per cent in 1986; see Figure 23). The bulk of transfer spending is directed at formal sector workers and their dependents. Their coverage includes pensions, health care, maternity benefits, occupational injury, sickness insurance and disability. Most of the growth in social spending has been for pensions for formal sector workers. The share of GDP spent on pensions rose from 1.9 per cent to 3.4 per cent in 1994). A few non-work-related benefits are also available. These consist of social assistance and health care coverage for some very needy people. Spending on this is very small, however. Social assistance and welfare accounted for 0.2 per cent of GDP in 1986 and for 0.3 per cent of GDP in 1994.

Figure 23. **SOCIAL EXPENDITURES**

As per cent of GDP

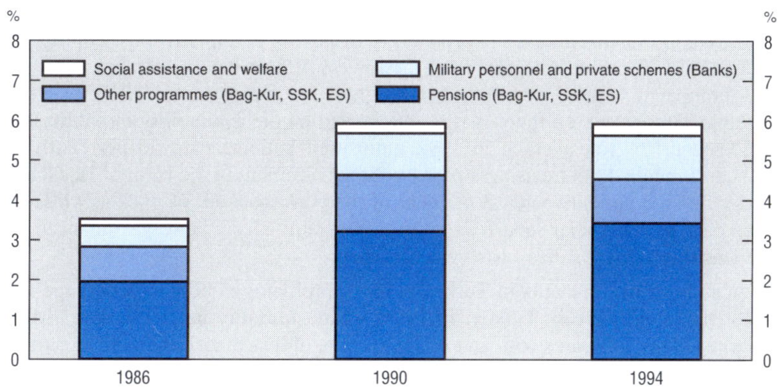

Note: Bag-Kur is the social insurance system for the self-employed; SSK (Soysal Sigortalar Kurumu) for workers in formal sector enterprises and ES (Emekli Sandigi) for civil servants.
Source: ILO, Social Security Department.

In 1994, 46 per cent of total employment, and 81 per cent of the total population, adhered to the public social insurance system – through SSK (workers' contributions), Bag-Kur (for the self-employed) and ES (for civil servants). These schemes' relatively low coverage rate is due principally to the fact that eligibility depends on having an attachment to the formal workforce. In principle, contributions to these schemes are mandatory for formal sector workers and firms (see Box 2 for a discussion of compliance problems among contributors). Also, most paid agricultural workers or self-employed farmers have to contribute to these schemes, but, in practice, few do.

(continued on next page)

(continued)

As just noted, programmes that target the poor absorb little of Turkey's social spending. For most social assistance schemes the threshold income level that determines eligibility is very low. The Green Card programme health care to people whose monthly earnings are less than a third of the minimum wage (TL 5 500 000 net per month at the end of 1995, which was worth about $90 at that time). The number of Green Card holders rose from 3.8 million in 1994 to 4.9 million in the first quarter of 1995. Under the social assistance and solidarity scheme (SAS), benefits in kind and lump-sum payments (rather than regular income support) are provided to certain, very needy people on a discretionary basis. Benefits are low and SAS recipients are expected to look for work. Another programme – the old age and disability assistance scheme – provides basic support for some poor people. By 1994, the programme's 842 578 beneficiaries received a monthly benefit of less than 14 per cent of the minimum wage (ILO Social Security Department). In addition, there are a few other discretionary schemes providing meals or cash benefits.

Access to medical care is highly uneven in Turkey and depends mainly on attachments to the formal labour market. In 1994, about 64 per cent of the total population had medical coverage under a public scheme. The OECD average for such coverage is 94 per cent (OECD, 1993). In Turkey, the probability of having health coverage is proportional to income: only 19 per cent of people in the lowest fifth of income earners were insured in 1992, compared with 83 per cent in the highest income category (AHIC, 1996). The uninsured in Turkey rely on their own resources and on the availability of public services at subsidised prices (on average in 1992, uninsured patients paid 56 per cent of their medical costs, while 44 per cent was paid by the government in the form of less than full-cost fees). Insured patients paid 23 per cent of medical costs out of pocket, while 33 per cent was paid by the social security system and, again, 44 per cent was financed by the government through subsidies on service charges.

Indicators of health status in Turkey point to problems in both the coverage and the quality of the health care in Turkey. In 1993, infant mortality per 1 000 live births was 62 in Turkey. This compares with an OECD average of less than 7 and with an average of 36 for upper middle income developing countries (World Bank, 1995). The under-5 mortality per 1 000 live births was 84, much higher than in any other OECD Member country, and even higher than the world average of 75. Although such outcomes cannot be attributed exclusively to formal health systems, there would appear to be significant room for improvement.

tax enforcement would involve public sector reform leading to more effective provision of basic government services used by businesses.

The transfer system in Turkey provides benefits mainly for formal sector workers. Box 5 describes the system of social transfers and health insurance. It shows that transfers are dominated by pension payments to formal sector employees. Despite generally favourable demographic developments, the pension schemes have required substantial injections of public money in recent years (see Box 2). Social assistance and welfare payments are very small (about 0.3 per cent of GDP in 1994). Those who are arguably most vulnerable because their source of income is from casual or irregular employment or who are working on their own account – particularly in agriculture or in the informal sector – do not usually benefit from social security insurance coverage.

Increasing the knowledge base, efficiency and innovation capacity

Upgrading skills and competences

This is an area where further efforts by policy makers would yield significant returns. Successful reform in this area would help improve welfare and would facilitate Turkey's transformation into a more sophisticated, advanced economy. Although Turkey has made some progress in this area, the financial resources devoted to the sector seem inadequate, especially in view of recent and planned increases in enrolment rates and in the length of compulsory schooling. Indeed, educational expenditure actually declined as a percentage of GDP over the 1965-94 period. Table 19 shows that public education and training expenditure accounted for about 3.7 per cent of GDP in 1965 and for only 3.1 per cent in 1993. The latter compares with an OECD average of 5.8 per cent. The share of education in the budget was 17.1 per cent in 1990, which represents a decline from 19.4 per cent in 1965. The share of education in the budget for the OECD as a whole was 13.4 per cent in 1990.

Turkey's performance in terms of literacy lags behind its OECD neighbours in the Mediterranean basin and significantly behind some countries with similar national incomes (see Table 20). In 1990, overall illiteracy stood at 19.3 per cent. Youth illiteracy (among 15 to 19 year olds) stood at 9.4 per cent in 1990, which is much higher than in Mexico (4.1 per cent), Portugal (0.7 per cent) and Spain (1.0 per cent). However, progress in reducing the total number of illiterate people has been substantial (there was a 38 per cent reduction over the 1970-90 period). Compulsory schooling still lasts only five years in Turkey,[94] but enrolment rates for the compulsory years are now above 100 per cent because of older persons still going to school. The enrolment rate drops off sharply at the end of compul-

Table 19. **Public educational expenditure**

Percentage

	Share of GNP			Share of public budget		
	1965	1980	1990	1965	1980	1990
Turkey	**3.7**	**2.8**	**3.1**	**19.4**	**10.5**	**17.1**
Middle East and North Africa	3.9	4.9	5.7	14.4	12.5	15.6
East Asia Pacific	3.2	3.5	3.5	15.1	13.2	15.3
Latin America, Caribbean	3.6	4.5	4.1	17.4	16.5	14.9
OECD	4.6	5.9	5.8	15.9	14.1	13.4

Source: Tansel, A. and A. Kazemi (1995), ''Equity in Educational Expenditures in the Middle East and North Africa'', and State Planning Organisation for 1990 public budget data.

sory studies, however (35 per cent of students drop out after the fifth year of school).

Like some other member countries, Turkey has difficulty providing effective educational services to children from disadvantaged socio-economic backgrounds. In some rural areas and among poor urban families, low or sporadic school attendance can occur because the child is employed or because the family in question does not see school as contributing to the child's or the family's welfare. Although child labour in Turkey is apparently not a widespread problem (relative to the few other countries with comparable statistics), it is a problem for

Table 20. **Comparative literacy indicators, 1990**

	Illiteracy rate, age 15 and over			Illiteracy rate age 15-19	% change of number of illiterates, 1970-90
	Total	Male	Female		
Selected countries					
OECD					
Turkey	**19.3**	**10.3**	**28.9**	**9.4**	**–28.3**
Greece	6.8	2.4	10.9	0.2	–45.7
Italy	2.9	2.2	3.6	0.7	–44.4
Portugal	15.0	11.2	18.5	0.7	–35.2
Spain	4.6	2.6	6.6	1.0	–34.3
Mexico	12.7	10.5	14.9	4.1	2.2
Non-OECD					
Algeria	42.6	30.2	54.5	12.2	10.6
Egypt	51.6	37.1	66.2	35.5	27.0
Thailand	7.0	3.9	10.1	0.6	–34.0

Source: World Education Report 1991.

specific (very poor) families. The results of a recent survey on child labour performed in Turkey are described in Box 6. For the time being, little use has been made of incentives for encouraging families – especially very poor families – to keep their children in school.[95] There also appears to be relatively little use of school infrastructure for delivering other social services (such as child nutrition programmes). Enlargement of such programmes might provide incentives for some families to increase their children's school attendance.

Since Turkey does not yet participate in international comparative testing – and indeed there is no systematic testing of students in Turkey – it is impossible to evaluate how much Turkish students learn.[96] There are some indications that, despite the rising enrolment rates, there may be problems. For example, shifts in the location of school infrastructure have not kept pace with rapid rural-urban migration and, in general, the geographic distribution of school infrastructure could be improved.[97] The average student-to-teacher ratio in primary schools in urban areas is 60 to 70 students, which is about twice the OECD average. Teachers' salaries are low and other aspects of the management of the teaching staff – training, non-wage motivational devices, etc. – could be developed further.

The tertiary education system enrolled 20.4 per cent of the 18-21 year age cohort in 1992 and 13.9 per cent of the 22-25 year age cohort (OECD, 1995). The university is the principal institution in higher education. There are several types: public universities (46 per cent of gross enrolments), open universities and colleges offering distance learning (42 per cent of enrolments), and 2 year vocational schools (10 per cent of enrolments) (TÜSIAD, 1995*b*). The system has experienced fairly rapid growth in recent years and several public universities have been founded – mainly outside the principal metropolitan areas – as well as several private universities. Each public university and technical institute possesses scientific autonomy and is a separate legal entity (*i.e.* it is not part of the Ministry of Education). It is responsible for managing its educational activities, scientific research and publications.[98] In practice, though, the managerial autonomy of public universities is limited by public service requirements. Their current and investment budgets are established for the most part by the Ministry of Finance and by the State Planning Organisation. Nineteen per cent of total funding comes from tuition payments and from the sale of other services. They are also controlled by the Higher Education Council and two affiliated

Box 6. **Child labour in Turkey**

Turkey is one of the few members of the International Labour Office to have conducted a statistical survey on child labour (the others are Brazil, Ghana, India, Indonesia and Senegal). The survey was performed in October 1994 as a module of the national labour force survey (see Ogut, 1995 for a discussion of the methodology and results). The survey defines a "child" as a person between the ages of 6 and 14. The definition of employment is "all persons aged 6 and over who were economically active during the reference period for at least one hour and persons who did not work during the reference period for various reasons, but who have attachments to the labour market". Thus, it includes wage-earners, household workers, and unpaid family workers on farms. It does not include children doing housework that deprives them of the possibility of going to school (in this latter respect, it differs from the ILO definition of child labour).

The results show that 8 per cent of the Turkish children in the sample were economically active. Thus, the incidence of child labour in Turkey seems to be low, compared to the other countries with surveys. Using ILO definitions, 25 per cent of the children in surveys conducted in Ghana, India, Indonesia and Senegal were found to be economically active (ILO 1995). Turkey's lower incidence may reflect its higher level of average income and, possibly, differences in survey methodology. The Turkish survey also points to important differences in the nature of child labour in rural versus urban areas. The rural version appears to be somewhat more benign – the vast majority of the rural child workers combine farm activities with school and they work on the family farm under the supervision of their parents. Child labour in urban areas often involves work in small establishments or in bazaars or streets and often occupies more than 40 hours per week. The main statistical results of the survey are:

- **Family situation.** Poverty is the principal motivation for child labour. Yearly disposable incomes of the great majority of households with employed children was less than $3 096. [Turkey's per capita disposable income in 1994 was $2 193 and the average household size was more than 4.8 persons in 1990. From these data, it would appear that the average income of a family with working children was well under one-third of Turkey's average household income (SIS, 1994)]. Working children also tend to come from less educated households: 94 per cent of the parents of employed children have primary school education or less. This compares with a nation-wide average of 77 per cent for the total population of 12 years and older.
- **Education.** Eighty-seven per cent of the children in the survey were attending school. Of these, 23 per cent were engaged in housework (not counted as child labour) and 4 per cent were working. Of the children who were not going to school, 38 per cent were working, 32 per cent were doing housework and 29 per cent were idle.
- **Hours worked.** One third of the child workers are working more than 40 hours in a week. 81 per cent of children that are regular earners are working more than 40 hours per week.

(continued on next page)

(continued)

- **Rural *versus* urban areas.** The incidence of child labour was found to be much higher in rural areas. Four out of five of all economically active children live in rural areas. This reflects the concentration of child labour in agriculture. In rural areas, 16 per cent of children between 6 and 9 years old are engaged in economic activities. Forty per cent of the children woking in urban areas are engaged in manufacturing. In urban areas, boys are much more likely to work than girls.
- **Earnings and employment status.** Unpaid family workers represent the largest group of child workers (79 per cent), followed by regular or casual employees, with 19 per cent. Of those children who are paid workers, 91 per cent earn less than $29 per month. More than four fifths of the establishments where children work are unregistered.

organisations, namely the higher education supervisory board and the student selection and placement centre. Higher income Turkish families frequently send their children to foreign universities.

The formal system of vocational training encompasses both private and public activities. A one per cent training tax is imposed on firms in the formal sector, but they get a partial refund for the training that they provide for their own employees. The main channels available for vocational education are apprenticeship training, short term skills development courses offered by both public and private providers, and open universities and colleges. The share of vocational institutions in tertiary education is very small compared with that of the university sector (as just noted, vocational education accounted for only 10 per cent of tertiary enrolments). There are also many public and private vocational secondary schools. In vocational lower secondary schools, religious instruction tends to dominate the programme, while upper secondary vocational education provides mainly technical education. At the secondary level, there are indirect indications that the vocational system is, on the whole, working poorly. Specifically, the people graduating from vocational programmes tend to have very high unemployment rates (SIS, 1994). However, the absence of a performance evaluation system – consisting of standards, testing, skills certification and information systems on job market experiences of graduates – makes it difficult to evaluate the system.

Product market competition

Competitive forces are strong in many parts of the Turkish economy. The unilateral trade liberalisation undertaken in the early 1980s opened up large parts of the economy to international competition. In much of the economy, domestic competition is also strong. For example, the informal sector pays few taxes, is not bound by most regulatory constraints, and often faces relatively low start-up and exit costs. Therefore, competition within the informal economy is presumably fierce and the informal sector competes effectively with the formal sector in some activities.

Parts of the economy are nevertheless sheltered from competitive pressures. Foremost among these are the SEEs, which are subject to weak financial disciplines due to public ownership (see OECD, 1995). In addition, the SEEs are major providers of intermediate inputs (often at administratively determined prices[99]) and generally operate in oligopolistic or monopolistic markets. For instance, in 1993 their share of output was 76 per cent in mining (they had all of coal and 81 per cent of lignite), 52 per cent in petroleum and they held dominant position in a number of processing sectors such as tea (54 per cent), sugar (76 per cent), tobacco products (all) and petroleum products (76 per cent). SEEs are a significant presence in the economy: they accounted for some 10.2 per cent of GNP and 12.9 per cent of manufacturing value added during the 1989-93 period. This share has been stable since the mid-1980s.

Rents from weak product market competition may accrue to the workforce in various ways (as higher pay, higher perquisites or overstaffing). Overstaffing appears to be an important part of the story in Turkey. An indication of the amount of overstaffing can be obtained by comparing SEE's value added per worker with those of private firms in the same sector. In 1991, for example, the value added per worker of SEEs operating in textiles and apparel was 48 per cent lower than their private counterparts in the same sector. Likewise, SEE value added per worker was 72 per cent lower than that of private firms in wood products in 1991, 60 per cent lower in basic metal products and 44 per cent lower in paper and paper products (Erocal, 1995). Although such numbers need to be interpreted cautiously, they do seem to point to significant overstaffing in some areas. Thus, if the privatisation process is to convert SEEs into viable firms, large layoffs and a lifting of the restrictive employment practices that disproportionately burden SEEs will probably be necessary.

Technology and innovation

Although Turkey has made progress in developing science and technology infrastructure – through an extensive network of public research centres and agencies to support basic and industrial research – investment in R&D and innovation activities, particularly in the business sector, remains among the lowest in the OECD area. Total R&D spending in Turkey in 1993 accounted for 0.5 per cent of GDP (this is comparable to some other lower income member countries' shares but well below the OECD average of 2.2 per cent). The government sector finances a large share (two-thirds) of R&D while the business sector funds about 32 per cent (compared with an average of 59 per cent for the OECD area). Most research in Turkey is performed in the higher education sector (67 per cent) which also employs 72 per cent of total R&D personnel.

The government has increased support for basic and applied research with the aim of increasing R&D spending to 1 per cent of GDP by the year 2000 and it recently introduced R&D tax incentives for firms. While R&D tax incentives may help offset market failures, the development of financial institutions that support innovative activities in firms could potentially have a broader impact on technological development. The problem of financing innovation was until recently compounded by an outdated system of intellectual property protection. Recent changes in intellectual property legislation should help remove disincentives to R&D spending in firms, increase private returns on R&D, and improve patent activity. To date, the lack of R&D infrastructure has not prevented Turkey from gaining a comparative advantage in resource- and labour-intensive products, but weak investment in R&D could affect the longer-term competitiveness of Turkish industry.

Policies governing technology transfer from abroad seem to be broadly appropriate in Turkey. The economy is open to foreign direct investment and actively seeks out such investment. Thus, technology embodied in investment flows is not impeded by investment barriers. Despite this liberal regime, inward bound foreign direct investment – which ranged from 0.54 per cent and 0.37 per cent of GDP over the 1990 to 1993 period – has been well below the OECD average (OECD, 1996*a*). This is probably in part due to Turkey's macroeconomic and political instability. The use of licensing agreements for technology transfer has grown from 10 licensing agreements in 1980 to 707 agreements in 1992 (OECD, 1995). Most of these were for transfer of manufacturing technology, but banking and tourism licenses have acquired greater importance in recent years. Likewise, the Turkish patent system is accessible to foreigners and 89 per cent of the patents granted over 1980-93 period were to non-residents (OECD, 1995).

Recent policy actions

Many of the Job Study recommendations were conceived for countries with labour markets and institutions that are significantly different from those observed in Turkey. Thus, in some respects, Turkey does not fit readily into the framework laid out in the Jobs Study. For example, the scope for reducing work disincentives, for loosening wage rigidities or adapting employment protection legislation is more limited in Turkey than in many other member countries. As noted earlier, Turkey's labour market performance will be improved by policies that support Turkey's transformation into a more advanced economy and that promote the participation of a broad segment of its population in the economic development process. Some Job Study recommendations – especially in the areas of education, product market competition, and technology and innovation – focus on the policy requirements of this transformation process. They are summarised in Box 7. Since the publishing of the Jobs Study in 1994, Turkey has undertaken a number of measures that conform to the recommendations made there.

– *Product market competition.* The Customs Union with the European Union came into effect in January 1996. The details of the Customs Union are provided in Chapter III. Briefly, Turkey is in the process of adopting the EU common customs tariff rates against third countries and has eliminated all customs duties and quantitative restrictions in industrial products *vis-à-vis* the EU. Turkey has also committed itself to adopting EU competition rules, including measures regarding public aid, within two years. In late 1994, Parliament approved an anti-cartel bill as well as consumer protection legislation and measures to establish a

Box 7. **The OECD Jobs Strategy: Synopsis of recommendations for Turkey**

The OECD Jobs Study sets out a strategy based on nine recommendations for improving the ability of OECD economies to cope with structural change. These seek to enhance the ability of OECD economies to adjust and to adapt, and to increase their capacity to innovate and be creative. The nine policy areas were broad-ranging and included improving the macroeconomic policy framework and the creation and diffusion of technological know-how. With respect to labour and product market flexibility it identified the need for initiatives in the following areas: working time flexibility, the entrepreneurial climate, wage and labour cost flexibility, employment security provisions, active labour market policies, labour force skills and competences and unemployment and related benefit systems.

The applicability of many of these recommendations is more limited for Turkey than for most other Member countries. For example, many of the Job Study recommendations dealing with increasing wage flexibility, reducing wage and labour costs and reforming employment security legislation and benefits systems are largely irrelevant for Turkey's informal sector (though they may have some relevance for parts of Turkey's formal sector). The principal requirements for better labour market performance in Turkey focus instead on improving the overall performance of the economy. In this respect, the first Job Study recommendation – dealing with macreconomic policy – is of particular relevance to Turkey, which has an urgent need to control its high public deficits and inflation (see Chapter II). Other Job Study recommendations – improving labour force skills and competences, reinforcing product market competition and enhancing the creation and diffusion of knowledge – are also relevant for Turkey, whose foremost structural policy challenges are to strengthen the institutional foundations needed to transform itself into an advanced economy and to promote the participation of broad segments of its population in economic progress.

Following from the more detailed review of labour market and employment performance made in previous sections, this chapter identifies the need for Turkey to move ahead in the following areas:

Improve labour force skills and competences

– Further economic progress for Turkey will require continuous improvement in human capital, with particular emphasis on *improving the quality of basic education* and *increasing enrolment rates*. Improvement in health outcomes, especially for the poorer elements of the population with inadequate access to *health coverage,* would also have beneficial effects on human capital formation.

(continued on next page)

(continued)

Increase product market competition

- Active pursuit of the *privatisation* programme and restructuring of State economic enterprise should be assigned a very high priority. The Privatisation Law passed at the end of 1994 is a step in the right direction.
- Further enhance domestic competition and accelerate structural adjustment by *extending the reforms in the competition law* passed at the end of 1994.

Reform of the Unemployment Insurance and related benefits systems

- Restructuring will require significant further employment shifts in parts of the Turkish economy, including ongoing movement of people out of agriculture. Once reform is undertaken, there may also be some labour shedding among uneconomic SEEs. If compensating displaced workers is considered to be politically expedient, then Turkey should take care not to burden itself permanently with an expensive programme for what is essentially a temporary adjustment problem. If Turkey wishes to accord high priority to unemployment insurance as a social objective, care should be taken to reduce the adverse work and job search incentives that such insurance/transfer schemes frequently entail.

Reform employment security provisions

- This recommendation applies to formal sector employment and especially to the State Economic Enterprise (SEE) sector. The principal measure for promoting job security is mandatory severance payments. These payments can be high and were originally intended as a kind of lump sum unemployment insurance. Notification for dismissal is also required (as a rule, it varies between 2 and 8 weeks, but may be longer). Because of unequal enforcement between the public and the private parts of the formal sector (in the informal sector such protection is non-existent) these requirements reduce the flexibility of the SEEs and promote the creation of an entrenched group of SEE ''insiders''.

Reform tax and benefit systems

- Formal sector workers are currently the primary beneficiary of social expenditure programmes. But their earnings are also subject to tax wedges that are among the highest in the OECD area. Reducing these wedges through both further tax reform and broader public sector reform would draw larger numbers of informal workers into the formal economy. Besides broadening the tax base, such an initiative would also increase the number of workers who benefit from improved social protection.

competition board. Implementation of this legislation has been slow (the Competition Board, for example, has yet to be nominated).

- Some progress has been made in the area of *privatisation*. A new privatisation law was enacted in 1994. This attempted to strengthen the legal foundations of the privatisation programme and provided for job loss compensation. Recent privatisations have been mainly in the areas of agri-food, coal and iron and steel. There has been some public controversy concerning the transparency of the privatisation process. Large privatisations of companies have been stalled, largely due to legal and administrative delays. Questions as to the legal status and constitutionality of the privatisation programme continue to hinder progress.
- Initiatives have also been taken in the field of *education*. As noted, greater scope for private universities to enter the tertiary education sector has been created by allowing ''foundations'' to create universities. The recent successes in increasing enrolment rates during compulsory education have already been noted. In other areas, though, results have been more mixed. An effort to improve educational standards and certification is now stalled. Similarly, an attempt to improve standards of teaching and to provide greater access to computers in vocational education has met with almost total failure.[100]
- As part of its effort to raise R&D spending in the business sector the government has launched several new programmes to promote *technology and innovation* in firms. New legislation on intellectual property entered into force in June 1995. This extends trademark protection to services and harmonises the industry and commercial property system with provisions under the TRIPS (Trade-Related Aspects of Intellectual Property Rights) in the WTO and also with EU regulations (OECD, 1996*b*). In 1995 the R&D Assistance Programme, in co-ordination with the Scientific and Technical Research Council (TUBITAK), was launched to provide financial assistance for designated R&D projects. The programme will also provide low interest loans for R&D projects through the Technology Development Foundation of Turkey (TTGV). Legal arrangements are being made to increase the participation of academics in industrial research projects.

Assessment and scope for further action

There are many grounds for optimism about the Turkish economy: it has a resourceful population, a dynamic small and medium enterprise sector, and it occupies a central geographic position relative to both established and emerging markets. The main blemish on this otherwise favourable tableau is government policy, both macroeconomic and structural. There are signs (*e.g.* the slowdown in urban job growth) that periodic fiscal and exchange rate crises are taking their toll on the economy. Some recent actions by the government represent steps in the direction of reform, however. The most important of these is the Customs Union, which should have far-reaching and beneficial effects on the Turkish economy. Much more remains to be done, however. The need for prompt action on a broad front is made all the more pressing by the progress on structural reform made by many of Turkey's competitors in world markets. Thus, Turkey will have to continue to move forward just to keep abreast of developments in other countries.

Many elements of structural policy over the last ten years have hurt, rather than helped, Turkey's economic performance. Public management is one of these and progress on public sector reform has been disappointing. Although a few divestitures have taken place, the privatisation process is largely at a standstill. In the area of social services, targets for health care and other social services have not been met (SPO, 1995). In issuing the new 5-year plan, the Turkish authorities have set out a blueprint for ambitious reforms (see Chapter III), but one that largely reiterates the unrealised goals of the previous plan. Making progress on significant parts of this agenda should be given very high priority in the future.

Education is another area where performance has lagged. As noted earlier, the 10 per cent youth illiteracy rate in 1990 is a key indicator of the problems. The latest Five Year Plan recognised these problems and accords high priority to education reform, however. It sets a goal of 100 per cent enrolment rates for what is slated to become 8 years of compulsory education and 75 per cent enrolment rates for secondary school. Higher education enrolments are scheduled to rise to 31 per cent.[101] The authorities also plan to improve vocational education by encouraging "school-business co-operation". An examination and certification system is to be established and a "Professional Standards Institution" founded. The occupation of teaching is to be made "more attractive" and the system of teacher training will be restructured to provide training in post-graduate educational academies. Universities will be given further autonomy and arrangements will promote further competition within tertiary education. These all appear to be reasonable goals, but OECD experience shows that reform, especially in a diverse country such as Turkey, may be difficult to implement.[102] Progress will require significant further investments of resources in education and a concerted effort by government officials, education professionals and other private and public institutions involved with education. Education reform is a slow process that often only bears fruit after many years. Turkey is right to make it a top priority and should advance as quickly as possible, especially in areas that will provide basic education for social groups that are otherwise likely to be left behind by Turkey's ongoing economic development.

The Five Year Plan also features several proposals for deepening and extending Turkey's social safety net. These plans call for more comprehensive pension and health coverage, the creation of an unemployment insurance system and targeted aid programmes for specific groups. The Plan states that "achieving a fair income distribution and improving social welfare are the main objectives" of this effort (p. 212). These are admirable objectives for any society and perhaps especially for Turkey, which still has significant numbers of people whose basic needs are not being met. At the same time, though, the public sector borrowing requirement is high (6.5 per cent of GDP in 1995). If Turkey's equity and social service objectives are to be realised within a context of sound public finance, then some difficult choices are going to have to be made between different programmes and between different social groups.

Further reform of taxation would have positive direct and indirect effects on labour markets. One set of reforms would seek to attract a larger share of the informal economy into the formal economy. The tax wedge facing formal-sector Turkish employees is among the highest in the OECD. This reflects low compliance rates, which shift a disproportionate share of the tax burden on to the comparatively small number of formal-sector workers. As shown in this chapter, though, they are also the principal beneficiaries of the deficit-ridden social security system, which is in urgent need of reform. Hence, tax reform designed to widen the tax base and increase compliance rates needs to be accompanied by broader public sector reform. If successful in drawing workers into the formal sector, such reforms would also have the advantage of increasing the number of workers covered by social and legal protection. A second set of reforms would seek to reduce further the array of tax exemptions and special concessions offered in many parts of the tax code. In addition to reducing tax distortions and easing administration, broadening the tax base in this way might provide scope for reducing the tax burden on formal-sector workers.

The planned introduction of an unemployment insurance scheme is a particular concern in this respect. OECD experience has underscored the need for caution when attempting to introduce unemployment insurance. Among member countries, there are few (if any) examples of unemployment insurance schemes that are actuarially neutral. Two separate objectives for introducing such a scheme in Turkey have been cited. First, the scheme is seen as a way of reducing the political resistance to structural reform by workers – especially in SEEs – who are likely to be adversely affected by it. Although compensation of these workers may indeed be politically expedient, it should be done so as not to burden Turkey permanently with an expensive programme addressing what is essentially a temporary adjustment problem. In fact, the privatisation law enacted in 1994 already provides temporary compensation for workers who are laid off because of privatisation. The second objective would be to enhance the general coverage and scope of the social safety net, of which unemployment insurance could be an important part. It is worth noting that an unemployment insurance scheme would benefit only workers in the formal sector. These workers already enjoy high social benefits relative to workers in the informal sector.[103] When budget constraints become binding, the Turkish political process will have to recognise that spending more on unemployed formal-sector workers means that less is available to spend on other worthy programmes (research, education, health) and on other worthy groups (for example, the very poor who currently account for only a very small share of social spending).

V. Conclusions

The Turkish economy remains influenced by the aftermath of the 1994 financial crisis. Following years of fiscal laxity and high inflation, the April 1994 stabilisation programme nearly halved the public sector borrowing requirement (PSBR) to 8 per cent of GDP, greatly reduced domestic demand and brought the current external account into surplus. However, inflation rose to well over 100 per cent throughout the last nine months of 1994, reflecting the earlier sharp drop in the Turkish lira and big increases in public sector prices. Stabilisation efforts were sustained up to September 1995, and economic trends remained broadly favourable. The economy recovered strongly in 1995 and inflation fell, while the current account was in balance. The consolidated budget deficit was on track. But real interest rates remained high, as economic activity strengthened and the Treasury floated larger proportions of domestic securities to finance the PSBR, thereby encouraging a switch into high-yield, Turkish lira assets and further capital inflows. The real exchange rate appreciated through much of 1995. Even so, international reserves were rapidly built up, and growth of the monetary aggregates accelerated sharply despite efforts by the Central Bank to drain liquidity.

Latent pressures on the economy became more evident after September 1995, with the announcement of early elections for 24 December. Restraint on public sector pay, farm subsidies and government transfers eased in the run-up to the elections. At the same time, administrative price increases were postponed and the privatisation programme ground to a virtual halt. Against a backdrop of a reversal in short-term capital inflows and a widening fiscal deficit, the Central Bank abandoned its earlier attempt to use the exchange rate as a quasi nominal anchor. Rapid money growth nonetheless continued, although its sources switched; international reserves fell, while domestic credit extended to the government rose sharply. In the end, financial market uncertainty persisted after the elections, as no single party obtained a Parliamentary majority. A (centre-right minority coalition) government was formed only in March 1996, but resigned in early June. Another coalition government (including the Refah (Welfare) and True Path parties) was formed in July.

This on-going policy hiatus proved costly in terms of Turkey's stabilisation efforts. With political uncertainty deepening, the Treasury was able to fund the PSBR during the last months of 1995 only through Central Bank advances and by issuing very high yield 3-month bills, embodying a very high risk premium. This raised domestic debt service substantially, with spillover effects on to 1996 budget prospects. Wholesale price inflation began to pick up from September and accelerated into early 1996. The current account shifted into deficit in the last two months of 1995 owing to a surge in imports, though invisibles earnings held up well and export competitiveness remained strong – by end-year the real effective exchange rate still remained some 20 per cent below its pre-1994 crisis level. In the end, real GDP growth was 7.3 per cent in 1995, far higher than expected. And, while the PSBR to GDP ratio was held to some 6½ per cent, about half a point higher than programmed, it was some 50 per cent higher in nominal terms – as was the final inflation outcome for 1995.

Despite a history of large fiscal deficits, Turkey's total public sector debt was less than 50 per cent of GDP at the end of 1995, reflecting the high degree of monetary financing of past deficits, and erosion of the real domestic debt stock by higher than expected inflation. However, such a process has limits, which may be close to being reached. Lenders now demand substantial risk premia on Turkish lira debt to guard against inflation surprises. As a result, debt service is expected to rise to over 10 per cent of GDP in 1996, absorbing over a third of total budget spending. Even with a small primary budget surplus, such debt service costs imply significant levels of new borrowing, which, if bond-financed, risks higher interest rates, and, if money-financed, risks accelerating inflation. Such an inflation, interest-rate nexus can only be resolved by running sustained primary budget surpluses to build credibility in the fiscal programme, which would then help to reduce the risk premia demanded on government debt.

The authorities' problem here is that the revenue base may be inadequate to raise the primary surplus sufficiently to outweigh the extraordinarily high real interest rates that are the price to be paid for past fiscal laxity. Turkey's tax base, especially on direct tax, is too narrow (partly due to deep-seated inefficiencies in tax administration) – necessitating heavy reliance on indirect taxes (which further weighs on an already wide income distribution and weak social consensus). Widening the tax base would be the most equitable way of raising revenue.

Against this backdrop, the Turkish economy is, once again, at a cross-roads. In the face of a sharp increase in debt service costs, the budget is targeting a substantial primary surplus in order to hold the PSBR to some 7½ per cent of GDP in 1996. Successful implementation of the 1996 budget will be key – and the chances of this are better, as the revised budget is much more realistic than previous ones. Nonetheless, the task is challenging. In particular, the projected increase in revenue will require substantial effort, and high debt service costs will continue to be a heavy charge on the budget. Given these pressures, the OECD Secretariat's projections are based on a judgement that the PSBR may be held to some 8½ per cent of GDP in 1996 (1 percentage point higher than the PSBR implicit in the budget forecast). Concrete measures to restrain the growth of the monetary aggregates and to speed structural reform are also assumed.

On these assumptions, GDP growth is projected to slow to 6 per cent in 1996, and to some 5 per cent in 1997. Inflation is projected to average some 80 per cent in 1996, moderating to 65 per cent in 1997, while the current account deficit could rise to over 3 per cent of GDP in 1997. The margins of error surrounding these projections are large. External financing is not a near term constraint. The main uncertainty is the likely reactions of financial markets to the fiscal performance, spiralling debt-service costs and continuing political uncertainty. Failure to adhere closely to the revised budget guidelines could trigger a deterioration in confidence and economic instability. On the other hand, sharper declines in the PSBR, inflation and interest rates (than assumed by the OECD Secretariat) are not excluded, given the interactions between monetisation of the public debt and inflation outcomes. Expectations of an improved fiscal outlook over the rest of 1996 could raise the demand for domestic currency, thereby providing monetary policy with room for manœuvre.

To underpin such expectations it is essential to address the structural causes of high fiscal deficits, with a coherent medium-term programme – backed up with credible annual budgets which can be delivered (see below). Structural priorities in this respect are:

- widening the tax base, by improved administration and more effective sanctions and incentives; establishing the preconditions for greater horizontal and vertical tax equity;
- vigorous application of hard budget constraints on State economic enterprises (SEEs), as well as accelerating privatisation; and
- fundamental reform of the deficit-ridden social security and pension system (by raising effective collection rates and Turkey's extraordinarily low retirement age).

In parallel, government spending should be reallocated towards enhancing the development of human capital.

Initiatives have already been taken in many of the areas above. But most of these need quicker action. Once such essential measures were in the process of being put in place, the authorities could announce a medium-term financial strategy (MTFS) based on sustained primary budget surpluses. The revised 1996 budget is widely regarded as a litmus test. But given the legacy of past fiscal profligacy, what is needed is an objective assessment of economic prospects with clear indications of:

- central estimates based on the range of probable outcomes for key macroeconomic variables (GDP, inflation, the PSBR and the current account deficit) given normal errors of forecast; and clear indications of the authorities' tolerance zones;
- and ideally, an announced set of contingency plans, which would be triggered in the event of pre-specified fiscal shortfalls (including government hiring and spending freezes, mandatory spending cuts, pre-programmed increases in public tariffs or excise taxes, etc.).

Increasing the transparency of the fiscal process, with prior commitments for redressing eventual shortfalls, could help to build a consensus for internal budget discipline, reduce the scope for economic rent seeking, and ultimately enhance policy credibility. Establishing an independent body with a mandate to inform the public of the real costs and benefits of government intervention in the economy could also be a helpful step. Striking examples of the costs of subsidies are losses per worker in the state coal mines (in 1992) amounting to six times per capita national income, and the operating subsidies of the SEEs equivalent to some 50 per cent of the central government's education budget and 300 per cent of its health budget over the period 1978-91.

A MTFS framework (with short-term benchmarks) could also reduce the uncertainty attached to holding Turkish lira (TL) denominated debt, and help the Bank of Turkey to gain more effective control over its balance sheet. The OECD Secretariat's analysis of Turkish inflation underlines the central role of monetary variables, even in the short run; and implies that a MTFS could be an important step in giving the Central Bank effective control over money and ultimately over inflation. To be sure, the 1994 Central Bank Act imposes progressively tighter limits on the Treasury's use of Central Bank advances to finance government expenditure. Even so, the Central Bank will directly finance (*i.e.* monetise) 10 per cent of the budgeted increase in central government spending in 1996 (and 6 per cent in 1997). But after a decade of endemic high inflation, much more needs to be done to break its inertia and undo its harmful effects.

In a medium-term policy framework a nominal anchor normally plays an important role in bolstering confidence and bringing forth in time the benefits of disinflation. In current circumstances, however, it is difficult to identify an appropriate nominal anchor. A hasty decision in this regard is unlikely to be successful. An interim strategy is therefore called for in order to strengthen the authorities' hand and to prepare the ground for successful stabilisation once the fiscal situation has been brought under control. Such an interim strategy would comprise two pillars. One is to widen the margin of manœuvre to deal with temporary setbacks. This requires a further strengthening of the Central Bank's balance sheet, and improvements in debt management, including a more steady pace for issuance, and creation of new instruments so as to lengthen maturity and to bring about deeper markets for government debt. The other pillar of the strategy is to strengthen the pre-commitment of policy intentions to re-establish market confidence in near term policies. Statutory limits on Central Bank advances to the Treasury, important as they are, still leave a wide margin of uncertainty. The timetable for gradual reduction of these limits could be accelerated so as to establish an effective constraint, and this could be reinforced by setting binding annual upper limits on Central Bank domestic credit expansion. Such actions can contribute to clarifying the monetary policy outlook and support the gradual restoration of confidence that, together with new debt instruments, should bring about broader markets for public debt and a reduction in interest rates.

Interest rates are only likely to be brought down in a durable way by sustained fiscal consolidation (which requires larger primary budget surpluses), vigorous structural reform and determined anti-inflationary policies. Once such preconditions are largely in place, there would be scope for increasing the average maturity of debt and reducing debt service costs. Greater, albeit prudent recourse to official foreign borrowing could be contemplated, as net long-term foreign capital inflows have been small or negative over the past decade. The government has recently floated 5 year Deutschemark and Samurai bonds at yields of 7.5 and 5.7 per cent respectively. Though expensive compared with rates paid by other sovereign borrowers, these rates are substantially below "real" domestic borrowing costs, except in the improbable event of a further extremely large real devaluation of the Turkish lira.

If clear and credible commitments could be made on maintaining primary budget surpluses, there would be a good case for issuing a proportion of medium and longer-term maturity TL bonds indexed to inflation or to the foreign exchange rate. Such innovations in debt management could have a positive effect on market expectations and confidence. On median forecasts of inflation, real rates of interest on 6 to 7 month Treasury bills are presently some 30 per cent or more, implying very high uncertainty concerning the short-term path of inflation. Indexation is clearly justified in situations where uncertainty threatens to become self-fulfilling. An inflation-proof TL instrument could be an attractive financial asset. It could provide the monetary authorities with greater scope for manœuvre by shifting some of the short-term foreign exchange deposits (held by domestic residents and banks) into longer-term instruments. It would also give the Treasury substantially lower "risk premia" on its debt, and would be a signal of the government's determination to address the economy's basic economic problems, without resorting to the printing press or excessive currency depreciation. Such an approach is not, however, a panacea. Should the government fail to put fiscal policy on to a sustainable path, it could be faced with a very expensive bill indeed.

The financial system is in the process of recovering from the 1994 crisis. Systemic risk has been contained, but deep-seated structural problems remain. Despite substantial financial market liberalisation since the 1980s, macroeconomic instability has stunted the depth and development of the domestic financial system – while enhancing the role of foreign currency assets. Turkish commercial banks in fact carry out comparatively few "basic" banking activities, *i.e.* intermediating between domestic savers and borrowers. The availability of bank finance recovered in 1995 but remains limited, owing to the elevated rates of return available in holding government debt and to the adverse effects of high inflation on financial intermediation. But this lack of financial market depth has drawbacks: it limits the efficiency with which savings are allocated to investment, and perhaps the level of national saving; it also restricts the Central Bank's control over liquidity in response to the ebb and flow of financial market confidence and short-term capital flows. As sound public finances are established and the role of financial intermediation grows, the need for better prudential control will also become more pressing. Improved auditing and accountancy standards have already been introduced, but transparency would be greatly improved by introducing accounting methods that would minimise the distortions caused by high inflation. Similarly, the open foreign-exchange positions of banks were limited to 50 per cent of their capital base, following the 1994 crisis. However, these regulations might well be reconsidered in view of the limited capacity of the Central Bank to act as a lender of last resort when a substantial share of activities is in foreign currency. The 100 per cent deposit insurance coverage for individuals might also be scaled back to limit moral hazard problems, now that financial market stability has been re-established.

Chapter IV of this Survey follows up the OECD's 1994 Jobs Study in a specific Turkish context. The major challenge facing Turkey is to provide jobs for its fast growing and rapidly urbanising labour force. Turkey's overall unemployment rate was 6.6 per cent in October 1995 (down from 7.9 per cent a year earlier); under-employment was reported at 6.4 per cent of the labour force. Despite breaks in series, the unemployment rate has been roughly stable since 1970. Turkey's labour market problems are only partly manifested in relatively high open unemployment. Rather, low wages, precarious jobs and jobs that do not build on human capital are important aspects of overall labour market problems.

Nevertheless, open unemployment is a problem for urban youth and women. Since the formal sector is quite small, informal employment and self-employment dominate employment relationships. Hence, wage setting for most workers is highly responsive to local, sectoral or macroeconomic conditions. Further, the public social safety net is rudimentary. There is no public unemployment insurance system and individuals face strong incentives to work. Unlike countries offering extensive benefits to non-working adults, unemployment is ''financed'' by families, many of whom fund fairly extensive search periods rather than obliging family members to take low paid or unsatisfactory jobs.

The jobs challenge facing Turkey is two-fold: labour market reform must concentrate on improving the economy's ability to upgrade the jobs on offer, while simultaneously upskilling the workers available to fill them. The most pressing general need is for fundamental reform to reduce or eliminate the role of government in areas where it does not have a constructive role to play (*e.g.* in SEEs); and to enhance its effectiveness in those areas where it does (such as public health and education).

Since the publication of the OECD's Job Study in 1994, Turkey has taken a number of steps that conform with its recommendations. The most important one was customs union with the European Union in January 1996. This will have far-reaching medium-term economic implications *via* opening-up the economy to greater world competition, foreign direct investment, and to better management and technology. Economic policy will also be affected in a constructive way through adherence to EU rules on competition, state aids and the importance placed on macroeconomic stability. Other positive developments include recent, albeit limited privatisations of some difficult large, loss-making firms, and the improved financial performance of SEEs. As regards education, enrolment rates have risen for the five years of compulsory schooling and worthwhile initiatives have been taken by the universities (including a new private university) to make them more competitive.

Although most of these recent structural initiatives are in the spirit of the OECD Jobs Strategy, much more needs to be done to improve Turkey's capacity to create more and better jobs, and to speed the pace of reform. In particular, the key human development objectives outlined in Turkey's 1995 Seventh Five Year Plan need to be attained. Proposals for lengthening compulsory schooling have been debated for years and should be implemented – along with accompanying increases in the education budget – with minimum delay. Likewise, faster privatisation – another long-standing policy objective – would free public funds for more constructive use, notably to improve basic health and education standards, where Turkey significantly lags other countries at similar levels of economic development. Finally, the high tax wedge for formal sector workers must be reduced through further tax reform and broader public sector reform. This would draw larger numbers of informal workers into the formal economy, thereby broadening the tax base and providing more workers with improved social protection

Several plans to introduce unemployment insurance are also under study and should be analysed carefully. In particular, if the plan is a part of a more comprehensive social safety net, its overall resource costs need to be assessed. OECD experience shows that plans based on premia paid by workers and firms and run by public agencies are rarely actuarially revenue neutral; *i.e.* they tend to end up being a drain on the Treasury. In an era of fiscal restraint, it is an open question whether expanding benefits to workers who already enjoy above average wages and social benefits constitutes the best use of Turkey's scarce public resources.

To sum up, against a background of continuing political uncertainty, 1996 may well prove to be one of most difficult, but critical years in contemporary Turkish economic history. Entry into customs union with the EU on 1 January 1996 is a significant step forward and is both a challenge and an opportunity. Successful implementation of the 1996 budget will be a critical test of the government's ability to restore sound public finances and lower inflation. The missing elements in a better medium-term economic performance remain reining in the PSBR and spiralling debt service, while establishing a smaller and more efficient public sector via vigorous structural reform. Further significant delays in structural reform and fiscal consolidation, at this juncture, risk exacerbating financial market instability and generating lastingly higher risk premia, thereby jeopardising economic growth. Conversely, determined efforts to meet the 1996 budget targets and accelerate structural reform could relatively soon result in a virtuous circle, thereby easing the heavy burden on Turkey's extremely dynamic private sector and helping the economy to realise its undoubtedly bright medium-term potential.

Notes

1. GDP data in Turkey are predominantly output based, with the expenditure components of GDP being imputed via an input-output table. Independent data sources for the income components of GDP are sparse. However, the new annual household income and expenditure surveys will eventually provide the basis for more complete household appropriation accounts. This restricted information base limits the internal consistency of GDP estimates, given the unknown (but apparently growing) size of the informal sector.
2. And a strengthening in the real exchange rate and delays in raising public sector prices may also have boosted spending by shifting relative prices in favour of the private sector.
3. Real wages in the private sector dropped by some 20 per cent in 1994. In the public sector, salaried workers experienced a 22 per cent drop, while wage earners had a 5.2 per cent fall.
4. Households and business are currently large net savers, leaving the public sector as the main borrower on capital markets. In this situation, higher interest rates may actually boost aggregate domestic demand in the short run, complicating the role of monetary policy.
5. National account estimates indicate that income from interest, dividends, rent and profits now exceed dependent wage income. This gap might be understated owing to under-reporting of non-wage income. Interest income is for example not subject to tax, though there are plans to include all forms of income (including interest income for persons earning more than TL 1.5 billion) in a unified tax base in 1997. Under this scheme only the real element of interest income would be subject to tax.
6. In particular, dependent employees represent only some 6.2 million out of a total working age population of 19.6 million in April 1994. While income and expenditure accounts of large private and public businesses are relatively transparent, those for the self-employed and small business (which make up the bulk of the population) are severely under-reported. Farm income is notoriously difficult to estimate. And Turkey has a very large number of firms with 9 or fewer employees; in part because firms of 10 employees or more are subject to more stringent administrative and tax and social security requirements. The results of Turkey's first comprehensive household expenditure and income survey will be released in late 1996.
7. Public sector price increases were quite high in the first quarter of 1996, following delays in raising administered prices prior to the December election.
8. Support prices for soft wheat, barley, rye and oats were raised by 94 per cent, while maize (119 per cent) and hard wheat (135 per cent) were raised more. But as support prices had

substantially lagged inflation in 1994, the 1995 support levels were still below open market prices and hence intervention purchases were minimal.

9. Data on income distribution are sparse. The forthcoming publication of the Household income and expenditure survey should provide a substantial improvement in the availability of data on this key issue.

10. In dollar value terms, imports of consumer goods rose 58.8 per cent, while capital goods and raw material imports rose by some 52 to 53 per cent, respectively. In part, this surge in imports may have reflected a hedge against a post-election devaluation by the incoming government.

11. Other invisibles earnings rose by over $3 billion in 1995 to reach $9.6 billion. The category of ''other'' invisibles includes freight income, transportation, financial and foreign trade services, official sector income, contractors' earnings, Turkish lira purchases from foreign exchange deposit accounts opened by residents and ''other'' items. Sixty per cent of the TL purchases from the foreign exchange accounts of residents with their earnings from abroad are estimated to be service income. Remittances from abroad relating to services for which details are unknown are classified as ''other'' items.

12. This debt is largely denominated in US dollar (36.8 per cent), Deutschemark (35.4 per cent) and Yen (19.4 per cent), with the remaining part in other European currencies and SDRs. This composition implies that its US dollar equivalent will rise (decline) when the dollar depreciates (appreciates) against other major OECD currencies.

13. Bond issues included 10 year JPY 10 billion Euro-yen bonds at 7.2 per cent in January, 5 year DM 500 million Euro-DM bonds at 5.7 per cent in February and 6 year JPY 30 billion Euro-yen bonds at 6 per cent in May. All these issues were completed under Turkey's Global MTN (Medium-Term Note) Programme. Also a 5 year JPY 75 billion Samurai bond issued at 5.7 per cent and a 3 year $500 million Euro-dollar bond issued at 8.25 were realised in May and June, respectively. The yield on the last Euro-dollar issue represented a spread of 210 basis points over comparable US government debt.

14. This also marked a milestone, as it allowed the Bank of Turkey to attain a net positive foreign exchange position, thereby facilitating its task of carrying out open market operations and its control of the growth of domestic assets.

15. See *OECD Economic Outlook* No. 58, Annex Table 29, December 1995.

16. High inflation erodes the ''real'' value of tax revenue due to lags in tax payments. At the same time, high inflation introduces large distortions into ''recorded'' profits. Inflation accounting is not generalised, but important steps have been taken to reduce distortions arising from high inflation: corporations and personal businesses can make full inflation adjustments on fixed assets in reporting sales income and depreciation; LIFO has been introduced in stock evaluation; partial tax deductability of the inflation premium portion of interest payments has been introduced to reduce the bias in favour of debt financing; and only the ''real component'' of interest income will be included in taxable income in the scheduled move to a unitary tax base in 1997.

17. The consolidated budget covers most of central government spending and revenues. The PSBR is a broader measure, covering borrowing by local administrations, state economic enterprises (SEEs), social security institutions and ''extra-budgetary funds''.

18. However, the dollar value of foreign currency debt still rose, reflecting the decline of the dollar *vis-à-vis* the yen and the Deutschemark.

19. In presenting the budget, the Turkish government assumed real GDP growth of 4½ per cent and inflation of 69 per cent in 1996.

20. A proposal to simplify the current excise tax system is being discussed by Parliament. More than ten current excise taxes would be replaced by a "special consumption tax", designed to improve the efficiency of excise tax collection.

21. Between May 1994 and mid-February 1995 the maximum maturity issued was 6 months, between March and August 1995 12 months, between October 1995 and mid-January 1996 5 months between April and June 1996 7 months.

22. As an example, assume the authorities start from a position of issuing 6 month bonds, which are spread evenly through the year, so that a sixth of the debt stock matures and needs to be refinanced each month. If then in January they are only able to issue 5 month bonds, these will mature in June, at the same time as the 6 month bonds issued in December, so that a third of the debt stock will need to be refinanced, instead of the usual sixth.

23. For example, while consumer prices should track changes in prices that are relevant to most households, the relevant basket for firms will be different.

24. Inflation, as measured by the wholesale price index, increased from some 22 per cent in the mid-1970s to 36 per cent in the period 1981-87 and 60 per cent in the 1988-93 period.

25. For an extensive analysis of the high inflation syndrome, see Heymann and Leijonhufvud (1995). Their study draws on the Latin American experience, as well as the European episodes of instability in the 1920s.

26. On the analogy of taxation, if the tax base becomes smaller it is necessary to increase the tax rate in order to collect the same revenue.

27. Previous Secretariat estimates suggest that a maximum level of seigniorage revenues would be attained at around 67 per cent consumer price inflation (see OECD, 1994, pp. 56-57).

28. In this respect, 1993 was an exceptional year as net transfers on long-term debt (which equal disbursements minus amortisation and interest payments) became slightly positive at the same time as short-term inflows and private long-term flows increased. The dramatic turnaround in net transfers on long-term debt between 1993 and 1994 – which the World Bank places at some $19 billion or the equivalent of nearly 11 per cent of GDP – undoubtedly contributed to the sharpness and depth of the 1994 crisis.

29. The statistics on sources of financing for the consolidated budget show the increasing role for Central Bank advances. Comprehensive data on sources of financing of the PSBR are not available for Turkey. During the 1980s, Central Bank advances amounted to the equivalent of 0.5 percentage points of GDP on average. This average excludes 1980. In that year Central Bank advances amounted to the equivalent of 2 per cent of GDP and inflation reached historically high levels of 120 per cent. Since 1991, Central Bank advances have taken on a larger role and have averaged some 1.8 percentage points of GDP over the last 5 years.

30. Measures included an increase in reserve requirements in January 1995.

31. Positive reaction to the April 1994 stabilisation programme and the announcement of a ceiling on exchange rate depreciation resulted in a monetary stance that was less tight than intended due to substantial reserve inflows. The stronger than programmed exchange rate towards end-1994 led to a reduction in the downside protection offered by specification of a ceiling on the exchange rate path. Currency substitution further complicated stabilisation efforts, as the easing of domestic interest rates coincided with a shift in market sentiment, linked to setbacks in attaining inflation targets and in implementation of structural reforms efforts.

32. Reserve money includes currency issued, banks' deposits with the Central Bank and other minor items. It differs from the monetary base by an amount equal to the Central Bank's money market operations (repurchase agreements plus liabilities in the inter-bank money market).

33. Net domestic assets equal reserve money, plus foreign exchange deposits of banks with the Central Bank minus net foreign assets of the Central Bank.

34. The banks, in addition to a large foreign exchange exposure, also carried substantial interest rate risk. Large movements in both the exchange rate and in interest rates caused large losses in some banks. The failure of three small banks lead to a contagion effect, large scale deposit withdrawals, a shift in deposits towards state-owned banks, and segmentation in the inter-bank market. Extension of deposit insurance to 100 per cent of all deposits by real persons helped to avoid a generalised loss of confidence, and the subsequent strengthening of banks' balance sheets has favoured a normalisation of conditions in money markets.

35. The nominal exchange rate experienced periods of appreciation during May and June.

36. Foreign exchange reserves increased from $9.2 to $14.6 billion between January and July. The monthly data show a peak at $16.7 billion in October 1995, although the actual peak occurred in mid-September.

37. As indicated in Table 10, the share of open market operations in the monetary base increased between December 1994 and September 1995 as the Central Bank drained liquidity by means of reverse repo operations and by intervening in the inter-bank money market.

38. The large increase in cash operations between December 1994 and September 1995 is linked to conversion of a substantial portion of the balance of the revaluation account of the Treasury into bonds. The balance of the advances account of the Treasury in fact declined in absolute terms between December 1994 and September 1995.

39. Prior to September, the Treasury had made no net use of Central Bank finance; by the end of December 1995, its cumulative use of finance amounted to some 1.3 per cent of GDP.

40. Equivalent to one-third the amount set as a ceiling for the year as a whole.

41. Growth of total Central Bank assets in the first quarter of 1996 was due to moderate expansion of domestic credit (at an annualised rate of 32 per cent) and strong expansion in foreign assets (at an annualised rate of nearly 170 per cent) linked in part to accelerated exchange rate depreciation.

42. In this regard, a further tightening of regulations concerning open foreign exchange positions of banks would not only have supported short-term policies, but would also have been a welcome development in a longer-term perspective.

43. Including attempts to pre-commit the government not to monetise the debt; such as indexing schemes for public debt issues.

44. This may include ranges for growth rates in balance sheet items under the control of the Central Bank under alternative scenarios.

45. The foreign exchange risk ratio is the ratio of foreign currency assets to foreign currency liabilities (domestic and foreign). The fact that the Central Bank has been mostly a net debtor in foreign currency has constrained its ability to conduct monetary policy and, even more so, to control the exchange rate.

46. State-owned banks account for a substantial share of total banking assets and have the most extensive branch networks. They also tend to have stronger links with non-financial state-owned enterprises. The shift in deposits towards state-owned banks in the wake of the banking crisis suggests that they are perceived to be less risky by the public, despite a lower capitalisation ratio.

47. First attempts at interest rate liberalisation came in the 1980s with deregulation of rates on loans and deposits. However, strong competition among small banks and un-regulated brokerage houses led to the re-introduction of controls in 1983 by the Central Bank. Partial deregulation took place in 1987 and full deregulation was accomplished in 1988. In the wake of the 1994 financial crisis, limits on bank competition for deposits were introduced, but these were abolished in January 1995.

48. Savings deposits refer to deposits by real persons. In this regard, the decision by Turkish authorities not to extend coverage to include deposits by large institutional investors is a step in the direction of establishing adequate incentives and market discipline.

49. See State Planning Organisation (1995).

50. For example, see *ibid.,* pp. 12-15.

51. An additional problem is that EU customs union has led to a loss of tariff and other foreign trade levies of some 1.2 per cent of GDP. Around half of these revenue losses have been offset by higher indirect taxes. Legislation to introduce a special consumption tax has been presented to Parliament. Its aim is to simplify and harmonise Turkey's complex indirect tax structure. Improving horizontal equity may be a necessary condition to tackling vertical equity questions through social transfers and targeted government programmes.

52. The company was restored to profitability in 1995, in large part because the workers accepted significant real wage cuts and more flexible working conditions, which would have been difficult to negotiate had the firm remained in the public sector.

53. For an inventory of privatisations and legal arrangements, see "Privatisation in Turkey: The Law and the Implementation", *Türk Ekonomi Bankasi Intermedia,* August 1995.

54. The Seventh Five Year Plan recognises the distortions caused by the current system of market price support, and calls for lower subsidies to inputs, improved productivity of agricultural research and development, and strengthening the role of producer managed

institutions in the market. Progress in these areas would have beneficial effects on both resource allocation in the agricultural sector and on public finances.

55. The reasons for slow structural reform and fiscal failure are complex. In a number of countries, the underlying causes appear to reflect a failure of governance capacity. A manifestation of this is the inability of the state to resolve conflicts between political actors (and constituencies), which intensifies conflict over distributional questions and the sharing of economic rents. In Turkey, such a situation evolved after the inconclusive December 1995 elections, with the protracted incapacity of the major mainstream political parties to form a coalition government, despite similar economic and political agendas. For an assessment of governance failures in a Turkish context, see Atiyas (1995). For a more general discussion of these issues, see Rodrik (1996) and Haggard and Webb (1994).

56. For a description of the role of the Australian Industries Commission, see OECD, *Economic Survey of Australia 1995.*

57. The Türkiye Taskörümü Kurumu (TTK), a state-owned coal mining company, lost $6.4 billion between 1985-90. In 1992 losses were $12 000 per worker or six times per capita GDP. At the same time, health and safety conditions were so bad that a miners' life expectancy was only 46 years, 11 years below the national average. For details on Turkish experience in SEEs, see World Bank (1995*a*), p. 33.

58. *Ibid.*

59. For example, the World Bank, *ibid.,* p. 192 cites overmanning at some 33 per cent for all SEEs and 40 per cent for the railways, based on comparisons using existing technology. The 1995 *OECD Economic Survey of Turkey* suggested that the same level of output could be produced with around one-half of the labour and one-third the capital inputs presently being used, based on reported TFP data for the largest public sector and private Turkish firms.

60. Indeed, the scope for cutting SEEs' deficits through improved management must be quite large, as it has been estimated that their deficits could be halved by merely cutting their costs by 3.5 per cent. See World Bank (1995*a*), *ibid.*

61. A World Bank study of a cross section of 13 developing countries, places Turkey along with India and Senegal as among the poor performers with respect to public sector reform. For details, see World Bank (1995*a*).

62. A broad based approach to structural reform may neutralise vocal resistance from ''special interest groups'' when reform has general but diffused economic benefits, but the costs of adjustment are borne by certain groups. Simultaneous reform can thus spread the burden of adjustment more fairly and may reduce distortions due to the sequencing of reform. This strategy succeeded in New Zealand. But the crucial difference with Turkey was the existence of a strong consensus among the inner political circles of power on ''the need for structural reform'' and an efficient administrative system. For an analysis of the New Zealand experience, see Douglas, R. (1980), and Douglas, R. and L. Callan (1987).

63. Turkey has made relatively rapid progress in deregulating domestic production and prices since 1980. But in 1994, administrative controls were still in place in some sectors, see World Bank (1995*a*), *ibid.,* p. 79.

64. For example, proposals for the introduction of an unemployment insurance system and retraining programmes to speed privatisation have been under study for almost three years.

It is now envisaged to present it as part of a package covering reform of the social security system including health care, pensions and unemployment insurance.

65. The EU abolished its quotas on Turkish exports of textiles and clothing on 1 January 1996, as Turkey was not filling these quotas and had passed the necessary legislation in conformity to EU laws with respect to intellectual, industrial and commercial property rights. EU rules applying to competition policy, including state aid will also have to be adhered to after a two year grace period, as will the progressive adoption of EU agreements on garments and textiles with third countries.

66. For a detailed list of other legal requirements and arrangements and an analysis of the EU customs union, see Sübidey Togan (1996).

67. The customs union covers manufactured goods (including agrochemicals) and the non-agricultural content of processed foods and feed. Protective measures on processed agricultural products are to be phased out by 1999. Both parties have agreed to work toward free trade in agricultural products implying that Turkey will in principle adopt the EU's common agricultural policy (CAP). However, moving towards a harmonised CAP system is fraught with difficulty. Turkey's high PSE is already a major distortion in the economy (34 per cent in 1994 and an estimated 23 per cent in 1995). Hence, aligning these to yet higher EU levels would exacerbate an already distorted situation, although the CAP might in the interim eventually be subject to reform.

68. Togan (1996), *ibid.,* Table 4. Calculations by the SPO gave similar results, with NPRs with the EU dropping from 8.3 per cent in 1994 to 1.5 per cent once the customs union is fully implemented.

69. The effective rate of protection is calculated as the difference between observed value added and what the value added would be under free trade, expressed as a per cent of free trade value added, see Togan (1996), *ibid.,* p. 19.

70. The standard deviation of NPRs drop from 20 to 14.5 per cent, while those for EPRs drop from 72.3 to 65 per cent, *ibid.*

71. Trade policies can have a substantial impact on economic performance. Following World War II, a large number of developing countries sought to accelerate economic development through massive import substitution programmes. These policies ultimately collapsed due to their massive inefficiency. But countries were slow to abandon this approach. Turkey was one of the first, although its reform was incomplete. By contrast, several east Asian countries turned to aggressive export-promotion with spectacular results. To be sure, these results also reflected other factors such as stable macroeconomic policies, high savings and strong emphasis on human resource development. But the catalyst for change appears to have been the re-orientation of trade policy. For a survey, see Urata, S. (1994) and Page, J. (1994).

72. For example, see OECD, *Economic Survey of Canada 1987/88* and *Economic Survey of Mexico 1992*. To some extent, these small gains depend on the closure rule adopted to maintain budget neutrality in the face of significant losses in tariff revenue. For a broader survey of regional trade agreements see Anderson, K. and R. Blackhurst (1993).

73. See, the *World Bank 1996,* pp. 57-60. These estimates find only a small 2 to 3 per cent depreciation in the real exchange rate from customs union. Hence, given the small size of assumed trade elasticities, the static impact of customs union is necessarily small.

74. In the longer term, the Multifibre Arrangement is to be phased out by the year 2004, at which time Turkey will face sharper third world competition in the EU market. Togan estimates that the EPRs for textile will drop by 26 per cent after customs union, but that for clothing will rise by 9.9 per cent. See Togan (1996), *ibid.,* Table 6.

75. *Ibid.*, Table 6.

76. For example, the TÜSIAD survey of its members indicated that 52.1 per cent of them regarded their sectoral competitiveness as high; 43.6 per cent as medium, while 4.3 per cent considered it to be low. See TÜSIAD (1995*a*).

77. Severance payments do exist and fulfill part of the role of an unemployment scheme.

78. Under-employment consists of three types of employed worker. First, there are people working fewer than 40 hours for economic reasons. If the worker is not in this category, he might still be considered underemployed for two other reasons: he may be seeking alternative employment because of insufficient income or he may be working in occupation that is not his ''usual occupation''. People who were looking for work because of insufficient income accounted for 76 per cent of the underemployed population (April 1994 survey), people involuntarily working less than 40 hours per week accounted for 23 per cent and people outside their usual occupation were less than 1 per cent. Although agriculture accounts for about half of employment it accounted for only 35 per cent of the underemployed in the April 1994 survey. Males are overrepresented in the population of underemployed (86 per cent) relative to their share of total employment (69 per cent).

79. Bulutay (1995), while noting the scarcity of reliable data on emigrant workers, summarises the findings of existing analyses. These show that workers emigrating after 1975 tended to have relatively high skill levels compared with earlier emigrants. This change appears to be associated with a shift in the direction of emigration toward Arab countries. He also notes that returning workers did not, on the whole, seem to have experienced significant upgrading of skills while working overseas.

80. The socio-economic characteristics of rural out-migration are described in Bulutay (1995). He notes that the typical emigrant was a young male aged 20 to 24. Typically, he moves to urban areas, often with the support of urban relatives. As the economic position of these initial emigrants becomes more secure – including, perhaps, the building of what are, in Turkey, fairly substantial squatter residences called *gecekondu* – other family members may follow. Thus, rural-urban migration tends to take place progressively (with families maintaining asset and activity bases in both rural and urban areas for extensive periods of time).

81. The unemployment rate for female youth (15-24 years old) seeking a first job in urban areas was 18.6 per cent in 1994 while for male first time job-seekers it was 13.2 (results of April 1994 survey). The total urban unemployment rate (for workers 15 years or older) was 19.6 per cent for women and 11.2 per cent for men. This compares with a rural unemployment rate of 1.9 per cent for females and 6.4 per cent for males.

82. Some families – principally in the poorer segments of Turkish society – appear to be under significant pressure to have all family members working. A recent survey by the Turkish

State Institute of Statistics quantifies the impact of this pressure in terms of child labour (defined as economically active people who are 14 years or younger). This survey is described in Box 6.

83. A union earns the right to represent workers in a given establishment by obtaining the votes of 50 per cent (plus one) of the workers in it. It must also have a membership of at least 10 per cent of the employment in the relevant subsector (of which there are 28, including agriculture, mining, energy and constructions, plus 11 in manufacturing and 13 in services). Such unions submit their requests for engaging in collective bargaining to the Ministry of Labour, which then rules on them. The unions may challenge refusals in the courts, though very few have in fact been challenged in recent years. The great majority of challenges have been refused in the courts.

84. The Turkish Employers Federation (TISK) reported that the share of union members among its members' employees fell from 81.0 per cent in 1979 to 69.6 per cent in 1994. This federation constitutes the core of Turkey's private formal sector and consists of very large employers who, taken together, accounted for about 2.8 per cent of all wage earners in 1993. According to one estimate, no more than half of these companies' unionised workers are covered by collective agreements (Erocal, 1995).

85. Little is known about how informal sector wages adjust to Turkey's inflation rate. Certain types of employment arrangements (*e.g.* day labour, self-employment) can be assumed to contain automatic corrections for inflation. Other types of employment (involving longer term relations) presumably require other forms of inflation adjustment.

86. As of December 1995, the minimum wage was TL 8 460 000 per month, which, after payroll deductions, was worth TL 5 500 000. At the December 1995 exchange rate (about TL 60 000 per dollar), the net minimum wage was equal to about $90 a month. This is well below the average manufacturing wages in both the private and the public sectors. The number of workers receiving the minimum wage or less is not known.

87. This annual growth is based on the following data: the number of civil servants (which rose from 1 460 000 in 1988 to 1 812 000 in 1994); labour costs per civil servant expressed in constant 1987 Turkish lira (which rose from TL 148 903 per month in 1988 to TL 302 119 per month in 1993). The source for the labour costs is the Division of wages of the State Planning Organisation. The source for the number of civil servants is Emekli Sandigi (the civil servants' retirement fund).

88. Involuntary separation rates (dismissals) are similar between the two sectors (an average of 2.2 per cent per half year in SEEs compared with 2.8 per cent in private companies). Other reasons (such as death, retirement, relocation and termination of temporary work) were also a bit lower among public sector employees than among those of private firms. Finally, it should be noted that there is significant movement between SEEs and private formal employment. In particular, SEE personnel have traditionally constituted the core of private business organisations' cadre of personnel.

89. This characterisation does not hold at all skill levels. People having very high level qualifications often find that salary levels in the public sector are low compared with those offered by the private sector. They might, therefore, prefer managerial and technical posts in

private businesses and, indeed, civil servants often leave government jobs for higher-wage posts in the private sector.

90. The relationship between formal and informal wages can be viewed from many angles. First, since earnings and employment in the informal sector probably react more quickly than formal sector wages and employment to labour market shocks, the informal sector probably acts as a buffer to the formal sector. For this reason, wage and quantity adjustments to external shocks are probably very strong in the informal sector and somewhat less strong in the formal sector. Also, since the skill mix demanded by the public sector is probably different than the skill mix generally available in the economy, it can be assumed that public employment influences the wage structure by raising the market clearing wage for some skills it demands relatively intensively. This effect is likely to be particularly strong if public employment exhibits significant overstaffing.

91. Private parties build constraints into employment relations in a number of ways. For example, employer-provided housing and pension arrangements that lock the employee into the firm are ways of increasing the employee's cost of changing jobs. The scope for building such constraints into labour relations in the informal sector is probably limited by the difficulty of contract enforcement that is a feature of any informal economy. To the extent that this is true, it probably means that informal sector firms do not engage in much training (since the incentive to train is related to the likelihood that the employee will stay with the firm after he has been trained).

92. Other examples of public services used by businesses are product labelling, grading and certification systems (in food and other areas where certified product standards are a necessary ingredient for the development of a more sophisticated sector) and protection of intellectual and intangible property (trademarks, patents, copyrights).

93. Family-run commercial operations or small family farms, for example, probably would never have enough to gain from entry into the formal sector to outweigh the disadvantage of having to pay taxes.

94. Increasing the length of compulsory schooling was mentioned as a high priority area for future policy action in the OECD's 1993 survey. At that time, the Government planned to extend the period of compulsory schooling, but it has not yet done so. The new Five Year Plan proposes to increase the length of compulsory schooling to 8 years.

95. See OECD, *Economic Survey of Mexico 1995* for a description of such an incentive programme.

96. Turkey has an examination system that determines university entrance and the group of students that aspires to enter the university system works to a standard that is set by that system. Inasmuch as the only exacting standard in the Turkish primary and secondary educational system is set by university entrance requirements, it resembles the US educational system described in the Survey of the United States, 1994.

97. For example, 12 000 schools out of 60 000 schools are working on a two shift basis.

98. The rector, the academic senate and the university administrative committee are responsible for the management of the university.

99. The OECD *Economic Survey of Turkey 1994* describes the close relationship between the SEE deficit problem and the settings of agricultural policies and, to a large extent, of

regional policy. About one-half of SEEs deficits are due to agricultural price supports. Other SEEs have an obligation to provide intermediate inputs to other sectors at below-market prices which also accounts for part of their persistent deficits.

100. This attempt to improve the teaching standards and equipment of vocational schools was financed by the World Bank. Problems were encountered at the managerial, logistic and human resource levels. The following recurring problems were noted: teachers felt that the use of the equipment did not fit easily into the curriculum; at times, the equipment delivered was not what had been contracted for; the people in the school did not always know how to install and maintain the equipment.

101. It also sets an objective of 16 per cent of the relevant age population for pre-school enrolments (actual enrolments were 5.1 per cent of the relevant age group in 1994-95).

102. See, for example, OECD, *Economic Survey of the United States 1994.*

103. As noted already, severance payments linked to tenure are required in the formal sector. These were originally intended as a lump sum unemployment insurance scheme. Unless these are removed, the unemployment scheme would represent an escalation of benefits for formal sector workers. They also enjoy health and pension coverage that is not generally available to informal sector workers.

References

ANDERSON, K. and R. BLACKHURST (1993), ''Regional Integration and the Global Trading System'', *Simon and Schuster.*

ATIYAS, Izak (1995), ''Uneven Governance and Fiscal Failure: The Adjustment Experience in Turkey'', Private Sector Development Department Occasional Paper No. 17, September, World Bank, Washington, DC.

AUSTRALIAN HEALTH COMMISSION AND INTERNATIONAL LABOUR OFFICE (1996), ''Reform of Health Financing, Pension and Social Assistance in Turkey''.

BULUTAY, Tuncer (1995), ''Employment, unemployment and wages in Turkey'', International Labour Office/State Institute of Statistics, Ankara.

DOUGLAS, R. (1980), ''There's got to be a better way'', *Forth Estate,* Wellington, New Zealand.

DOUGLAS, R. and L. CALLAN (1987), ''Towards prosperity'', D. BATEMAN (ed.), Auckland, New Zealand.

EROCAL, D. (1995), ''Jobs Study Follow Up – Turkey'', mimeo, TÜSIAD and OECD Economics Department.

HAGGARD, S. and S. WEBB, eds. (1994), ''Voting For Reform'', World Bank, Oxford Books, June.

HEYMANN, Daniel and A. LEIJONHUFVUD (1995), ''High inflation'', Oxford University Press.

INTERNATIONAL LABOUR ORGANISATION (1995), ''Child Labour'', Internet document.

INTERNATIONAL LABOUR OFFICE (1996), ''Social Security Final Report'', Geneva.

OECD (1993), *Health Systems,* Paris.

OECD (1994), *Economic Survey of Turkey 1994,* Paris.

OECD (1995), *Economic Survey of Turkey 1995,* Paris.

OECD (1996*a*), *Economies at a Glance: Structural Indicators,* Paris.

OECD (1996*b*), *Science, Technology and Industry Outlook,* Paris.

OGUT, N. (1995), ''Turkish Experience on Child Labour Statistics'', State Institute of Statistics, Ankara.

PAGE, J. (1994), ''The East Asian Miracle: Four Lessons for Development Policy'', *National Bureau of Economic Research Macroeconomics Annual,* pp. 219-280.

RODRIK, D. (1996), ''Understanding Economic Policy Reform'', *Journal of Economic Literature,* pp. 9-39, March.

STATE INSTITUTE OF STATISTICS (1994), ''Household Labour Force Survey Results, April 1994'', Ankara.

STATE PLANNING ORGANISATION (1995), ''Seventh Five Year Development Plan, 1996-2000'', Ankara.

TOGEN, Sübidey (1996), ''Opening up the Turkish Economy in the Context of the Customs Union with the EU'', mimeo, Bilkent University, Ankara.

TÜRK BANKASI, Economi Intermedia (1995), ''Privatisation in Turkey: The Law and the Implementation''.

TÜSIAD (1995*a*), ''The Turkish Economy 1995'', Turkish Industrialists and Businessmen's Association, Istanbul.

TÜSIAD (1995*b*), ''Higher Education, Science and Technology in Turkey and in the World. Executive Summary'', Turkish Industrialists and Businessmen's Association, Istanbul.

URATA, S. (1994), ''Trade liberalization and productivity growth in Asia: Introduction and major findings'', *The Developing Economies,* pp. 365-396, December.

WORLD BANK (1995*a*), ''Bureaucrats in business'', Oxford University Press.

WORLD BANK (1995*b*), ''World Development Report 1995''.

WORLD BANK (1996), ''Turkey Challenges For Adjustment''.

Annex I

Wholesale price inflation in 1995 and 1996

This annex analyses recent inflation outcomes, using the regression reported in Annex I of the 1995 Economic Survey of Turkey (reproduced in Table A1). This regression links the monthly change in wholesale prices to growth of the money supply (M2) and the depreciation of the Turkish lira/dollar exchange rate. The regression equation was estimated over the period July 1986 to May 1994, and included dummy

Table A1. **Regression for wholesale prices**[1]

Explanatory variable	Coefficient	T-ratio
Constant	–0.23675	1.0
Growth of wholesale prices (–1)	0.26149	4.4
Growth of exchange rate (TL/US$)	0.19639	3.0
Growth of M2	0.09969	1.9
Growth of M2 (–1)	–0.08115	1.2
Growth of M2 (–2)	–0.02982	0.5
Growth of M2 (–3)	0.08091	1.4
Growth of M2 (–4)	0.12769	2.3
Log (wholesale prices/M2) (–1)	–0.02292	1.1
Dummy for April 1994	0.13116	3.9
Dummy for January	0.02748	3.7
Dummy for June	–0.02874	4.4
Regression standard error	0.0162	
Diagnostic statistics[2]		
Serial correlation	F (12.71) =	0.75
Functional form	F (1.82) =	0.00
Normality	Chi-Square (2) =	30.26
Heteroscedasticity	F (1.93) =	0.11

Note: Growth of a variable is defined as the change in its logarithm.

1. Dependent variable: monthly growth of wholesale prices. Period: July 1986 to May 1994, monthly data.
2. The tests indicate that the regression error-terms are not normally distributed, but that the regression is otherwise well-specified.

Source: OECD.

variables to account for the tendency for wholesale price inflation to rise in January and fall in June in each year, and a dummy variable to account for the exceptional increase in wholesale prices in April 1994.

The estimated relation has the following features:

i) In the long-run, WPI inflation is determined by the growth of the money supply. WPI inflation adjusts to M2 growth with a lag of four to eight months: a 1 percentage point increase in M2 leads to a 0.32 percentage point increase in WPI inflation after four months, rising to 0.45 percentage points after eight months, 0.52 percentage points after a year, and 1 percentage point in the long run.

Table A2. **Regression predictions of monthly wholesale price inflation**

		Prediction	Outturn [1]	Error
1995	January [2]	6.8	8.4	–1.6
	February	5.3	7.1	–1.8
	March	4.3	5.6	–1.3
	April	4.2	5.1	–0.9
	May	3.3	1.9	1.4
	June [3]	1.6	1.3	0.3
	July	4.0	2.3	1.7
	August	4.7	2.3	2.4
	September	3.6	4.6	–1.0
	October	4.8	3.7	1.1
	November	5.5	3.5	2.0
	December	5.2	4.3	0.9
1996	January [2]	6.3	9.7	–3.4
	February	6.3	5.8	0.5
	March	4.8	7.0	–2.2
	April	6.8	8.1	–1.3
	May	5.0	4.1	0.9
	June [3]	1.5	2.7	–1.2
	July [4]	4.0	..	..
	August	5.3	..	..
	September	4.1	..	..
	October	3.6	..	..
	November	3.5	..	..
	December	3.4	..	..

1. The regression was estimated using wholesale price data constructed using 1987 weights. The monthly outturns reported here are from the new wholesale price index, using 1994 weights, but rescaled to 1987 = 100.
2. Predictions for January include an increase of 2.7 per cent from the seasonal dummy variable.
3. Predictions for June include a decline of 2.9 per cent from the seasonal dummy variable.
4. Predictions for July 1996 onwards assume growth of M2 of 2 per cent a month from June 1996, and exchange rate depreciation of 4 per cent a month from July 1996.

Source: OECD.

Table A3. **Money supply and exchange rate development**

Percentage change, monthly rate

		Money supply M2	Exchange rate TL/US$
1994	Q3	6.3	2.3
	Q4	2.3	3.1
1995	Q1	8.5	3.9
	Q2	8.4	1.4
	Q3	4.8	3.2
	Q4	4.1	5.7
1996	Q1	4.2	6.5
	Q2	. .	5.3

Source: OECD.

ii) Changes in the exchange rate have an immediate impact on WPI inflation. The impact of the exchange rate (0.20) is close to the share of imports in GDP.

iii) The coefficient on past wholesale price inflation implies relatively low inertia in monthly inflation, with temporary shocks to the price level having little impact on wholesale price inflation after two months.

Wholesale prices increased by over 5 per cent in each of the first four months of 1995, by less than 2½ per cent in the middle four months, between 3½ and 5 per cent in the last four months of 1995, were back above 5 per cent in the first four months of 1996, but declined again in May and June. The regression predicted these movements reasonably well, with an average under prediction of 0.2 percentage points, and an average absolute prediction error of 1.4 percentage points (Table A2).

The regression explains the resurgence of wholesale price inflation after September 1995 by strong money supply growth earlier in the year. In the first half of 1995, M2 grew by over 8 per cent a month, but slowed to between 4 and 5 per cent in the second half (Table A3). In contrast, exchange rate depreciation averaged less than 3 per cent a month in the first three quarters of 1995, but over 5 per cent a month in the nine months ending June 1996. On the assumptions that growth of M2 is held to 2 per cent a month from June 1996 onwards and exchange rate depreciation is approximately in line with wholesale price inflation, then wholesale price inflation is predicted to average around 4 per cent a month in the second half of 1996, equivalent to an annualised inflation rate of around 60 per cent (see Table A2).

Annex II

Medium-term deficit reduction and financing

Since 1994, measures have been taken to restore public finances, by reducing the large primary deficit and limiting the recourse to money finance. Substantial progress has been made, but the PSBR remains high ($6^1/_2$ per cent of GDP in 1995), entailing substantial demand on domestic savings. This situation, combined with uncertainty over inflation, has led to very high nominal and real interest-rates on public sector debt. Government spending on debt interest payments may rise from $7^1/_2$ per cent of GDP in 1995 to over $10^1/_2$ per cent of GDP in 1996, hindering attempts to reduce overall public borrowing.

This annex reports a number of simulations designed to illustrate what needs to be done to achieve sound medium-term public finances. The current high level of interest rates means that the government will need to target a primary surplus. The first simulation (Table A4) assumes that the public sector primary surplus is held at 2 per cent of GDP between 1996 and 2000. Achieving this would suffice to bring the public sector debt to GDP ratio down from 48 to 41 per cent of GDP between 1996 and 2000; debt service would drop from $10^3/_4$ per cent to $4^1/_2$ per cent of GDP over the same period.

A second simulation (Table A5) illustrates the same scenario, but with a primary budget balance of zero between 1996 and 2000. It is assumed that this would put further upward pressure on interest-rates, with the real interest-rate on domestic borrowing 2 percentage points higher than in the first scenario. By 2000, debt interest payments exceed those in the first simulation by $2^1/_2$ per cent of GDP, while the debt stock is around 14 percentage points of GDP higher, and is still rising.

Since April 1994, limited access to foreign borrowing and a reduction in money finance have necessitated greater dependence on domestic borrowing to finance public deficits. Lenders have demanded large risk premia to compensate for the uncertain real return attached to holding government paper. *Ex post* real returns have been generally very high. This poses a problem when the government attempts to brings down inflation: reducing inflation by more than investors expect leads to higher *ex post* real interest costs on its borrowing. This problem can be alleviated by issuing index-linked debt (see Chapter II).

The third simulation (Table A6) is a variant of the first simulation in which the government issues index-linked debt (with the index taken to be the CPI). This simulation

Table A4. **Public sector deficits and debts in the medium-term, scenario A**

	1995	1996	1997	1998	1999	2000
Assumptions						
Real GDP growth	7.3	6.0	5.0	5.0	5.0	5.0
Inflation (GDP deflator)	82	80	65	40	20	10
Real exchange-rate (% change, end year)	5	0	0	0	0	0
Interest-rates payable on						
Non-indexed TL debt, real	22	20	18	15	12	10
Non-indexed TL debt, nominal	122	116	95	61	34	21
Indexed TL debt, real	. .	10	9	8	7	7
Indexed TL debt, nominal	. .	98	80	51	28	17
Foreign currency debt, real	5	6	6	6	6	6
Foreign currency debt, nominal	7	8	8	8	8	8
Public sector primary balance (% of GDP)	1.1	2	2	2	2	2
Money financing of deficit (% of GDP)	1.3	0.9	0.7	0.5	0.3	0.2
Proportion of new borrowing in index-linked TL debt	0	0	0	0	0	0
Outcomes (% of GDP)						
Budget interest payments	7.6	10.8	10.2	8.4	6.2	4.6
Public sector balance	–6.6	–8.8	–8.2	–6.4	–4.2	–2.6
Non-indexed TL debt	18.0	18.3	18.7	19.1	19.3	19.3
Indexed TL debt	0.0	0.0	0.0	0.0	0.0	0.0
Foreign currency debt	30.2	27.4	25.1	23.5	22.3	21.3
Total public sector debt	48.2	45.7	43.8	42.6	41.7	40.6

Source: OECD.

Table A5. **Public sector deficits and debts in the medium-term, scenario B**

	1996	1997	1998	1999	2000
Assumptions					
As scenario A, except:					
Public sector primary balance (% of GDP)	0	0	0	0	0
Interest-rates payable on					
Non-indexed TL debt, real	22	20	17	14	12
Non-indexed TL debt, nominal	120	98	64	37	23
Outcomes (% of GDP)					
Budget interest payments	11.1	11.8	10.8	8.8	7.1
Public sector balance	–11.1	–11.8	–10.8	–8.8	–7.1
Non-indexed TL debt	20.5	23.7	26.9	30.1	33.1
Indexed TL debt	0.0	0.0	0.0	0.0	0.0
Foreign currency debt	27.4	25.1	23.5	22.3	21.3
Total public sector debt	48.0	48.7	50.4	52.4	54.5

Source: OECD.

Table A6. **Public sector deficits and debts in the medium-term, scenario C**

	1996	1997	1998	1999	2000
Assumptions					
As scenario A, except:					
Proportion of new borrowing in index-linked TL debt	0.33	0.33	0.33	0.33	0.33
Outcomes (% of GDP)					
Budget interest payments	10.8	10.0	8.0	5.8	4.3
Public sector balance	–8.8	–8.0	–6.0	–3.8	–2.3
Non-indexed TL debt	15.6	14.6	14.1	13.8	13.5
Indexed TL debt	2.6	3.9	4.5	4.7	4.8
Foreign currency debt	27.4	25.1	23.5	22.3	21.3
Total public sector debt	45.7	43.6	42.1	40.9	39.7

Source: OECD.

assumes that a third of new borrowing is in the form of index-linked debt, with lower (but guaranteed) *ex post* real returns. By the year 2000, debt interest payments are lower than in the first simulation by around ¼ per cent of GDP, even though the debt stock is only 1 per cent of GDP lower.

Issuing index-linked paper will only generate savings if inflation outcomes are substantially better than inflation expectations priced into non-indexed debt; and conversely, if inflation outcomes are substantially worse. This feature is illustrated in variants

Table A7. **Public sector deficits and debts in the medium-term, scenario A1**

	1996	1997	1998	1999	2000
Assumptions					
As scenario A, except:					
Inflation (GDP deflator)	80	80	70	60	50
Interest-rates payable on					
Non-indexed TL debt, real	20	5	2	2	4
Non-indexed TL debt, nominal	116	89	73	63	56
Indexed TL debt, nominal	98	96	84	71	59
Outcomes (% of GDP)					
Budget interest payments	10.8	9.0	7.5	6.3	5.3
Public sector balance	–8.8	–7.0	–5.5	–4.3	–3.3
Non-indexed TL debt	18.3	16.7	14.8	13.2	11.7
Indexed TL debt	0.0	0.0	0.0	0.0	0.0
Foreign currency debt	28.0	25.8	24.1	22.5	19.7
Total debt	46.3	42.5	38.9	35.6	31.4

Source: OECD.

Table A8. **Public sector deficits and debts in the medium-term, scenario C1**

	1996	1997	1998	1999	2000
Assumptions					
As scenario C, except:					
Inflation (GDP deflator)	80	80	70	60	50
Interest-rates payable on					
Non-indexed TL debt, real	20	5	2	2	4
Non-indexed TL debt, nominal	116	89	73	63	56
Indexed TL debt, nominal	98	96	84	71	59
Outcomes (% of GDP)					
Budget interest payments	10.8	9.1	7.7	6.6	5.6
Public sector balance	–8.8	–7.1	–5.7	–4.6	–3.6
Non-indexed TL debt	15.7	13.3	11.5	10.2	9.0
Indexed TL debt	2.6	3.5	3.6	3.4	3.2
Foreign currency debt	28.0	25.8	24.1	22.5	19.7
Total debt	46.3	42.6	39.2	36.1	31.9

Source: OECD.

of the first and third simulations, in which inflation outcomes reduce the *ex post* return on non-indexed debt below the return offered on indexed debt. In 2000, debt interest payments and the total debt stock are both lower if no index-linked debt is issued (Table A7) than if a third of new debt issued is index-linked (Table A8).

These simulations highlight an important issue – what proportion of index-linked debt should be issued. In theory, this proportion should depend on the likelihood that the *ex post* real return on non-indexed debt exceeds the guaranteed return on indexed debt. In practice, the private sector has been unwilling to bear the risk of holding non-indexed longer-term debt. A risk-sharing strategy suggests that the government should bear the risks associated with longer term debt, by issuing index-linked debt for maturities of a year or more. At the same time, the private sector would be left to bear the risks (and rewards) associated with holding shorter-term debt, by issuing non-indexed debt at maturities of a year and less. This mixed approach would also create a class of TL-denominated assets with longer maturities that could prove an attractive alternative to holding foreign currency deposits. Provided that progress is made in reducing inflation, the risk premium on non-indexed debt should eventually also come down. As this occurs, the proportion of debt issued as indexed debt should also be reduced.

Annex III

Calendar of main economic events

1995

January

Fuel taxes raised: on petrol from 70 per cent to 85 per cent; on kerosene from 66 per cent to 80 per cent; motor oil from 58 per cent to 70 per cent; central heating oil from 1 per cent to 25 per cent.

March

Turkey and the European Union agree details of a customs union to commence 1 January 1996.

April

Mass Housing Fund levies reduced by 20 per cent.

IMF agrees to extend the expiry of its standby agreement from September 1995 to February 1996, and provides additional loan of SDR 101.2 million ($57 million).

June

New tax law introduced. Designed to reform administration of tax collection, in order to enhance revenue collection.

Decree laws on protection of trademarks and patent rights issued, together with amendments to Turkish commercial code, as part of preparation for EU customs union.

July

Further reduction of 20 per cent in Mass Housing Fund levies (see April).

September

Minimum wage increases to TL 8.46 million a month gross (up 103 per cent), TL 5.5 million net (up 96 per cent).

The Republican People's Party (CHP) withdraws from the coalition government. Mrs. Ciller resigns as Prime Minister, but continues as caretaker Prime Minister pending formation of new government.

October

Parliament ratifies a supplementary budget for 1995, which authorises additional spending of TL 380 trillion. Revenues are expected to be higher by TL 276 trillion.

Parliament passes a provisional budget for 1996, authorising spending for January-April 1996, pending formation of a new government.

December

General elections held on 24 December. No clear winner. Mrs. Ciller continues as caretaker Prime Minister.

Privatisation revenues total $576 million in 1995.

1996

January

Turkey enters customs union with the European Union. Mass Housing Fund levies and tariffs on imports from the EU abolished.

March

Motherland (ANAP) and True Path (DYP) parties agree to form a coalition government. Mr. Yilmaz (ANAP) to be Prime Minister for remainder of 1996, followed by two years for Mrs. Ciller (DYP), the following year for Mr. Yilmaz, and a final year by a DYP deputy other than Mrs. Ciller.

April

Parliament approves budget for 1996. Consolidated budget deficit projected to be TL 861 trillion (6½ per cent of GDP), in a context of projected GDP growth of 4½ per cent, and inflation of 65 per cent in 1996.

June

Resignation of ANAP-DYP coalition government.

July

Formation of new coalition between Welfare (Refah) and True Path (DYP) parties. Mr. Erbakan (Refah) to be Prime Minister for first two years, Mrs. Ciller (DYP) for following two years.

STATISTICAL ANNEX AND STRUCTURAL INDICATORS

Table A. **Gross domestic product, current prices**

TL billion

	1986	1987	1988	1989	1990	1991	1992	1993	1994	1995
Private consumption	34 394	51 019	82 050	149 140	269 562	434 366	734 306	1 333 631	2 565 519	5 399 505
Government consumption	4 592	5 845	9 837	21 240	43 083	78 256	141 318	255 539	450 957	837 243
Gross fixed capital investment	12 745	18 491	33 738	51 837	89 892	149 272	251 435	505 866	946 185	1 786 276
Construction	6 354	11 727	22 559	36 103	57 388	95 425	159 138	301 655	588 157	962 730
Non-housing	3 585	5 392	8 700	14 672	23 555	40 694	66 343	121 707	229 222	351 732
Housing	2 769	6 335	13 859	21 431	33 833	54 731	92 795	179 948	358 935	610 998
Machinery and equipment	6 391	6 764	11 179	15 734	32 504	53 847	92 297	204 211	358 028	823 546
Increase in stocks	409	687	–1 247	1 522	6 601	–6 160	4 000	21 619	–121 416	3 834
Total domestic demand	52 140	76 042	124 378	223 739	409 138	655 734	1 131 059	2 116 655	3 841 245	8 026 858
Exports of goods and services	7 043	11 642	24 106	36 833	52 215	87 215	157 360	270 997	826 379	1 532 381
Imports of goods and services	8 104	13 267	22 682	40 420	69 042	104 819	189 646	383 358	788 530	1 888 011
Statistical discrepancy	0	306	3 424	7 172	749	–8 013	–5 405	–22 428	–10 666	–116 471
Gross domestic product	51 079	74 723	129 226	227 324	393 060	630 117	1 093 368	1 981 866	3 868 428	7 554 757

Note: In this annex, all GDP data refer to the new series of the National Accounts as published by the State Institute of Statistics.
Source: State Institute of Statistics, *Gross National Product,* and OECD, *National Accounts.*

Table B. **Gross domestic product, constant prices**

1987 prices, TL billion

	1986	1987	1988	1989	1990	1991	1992	1993	1994	1995
Private consumption	51 179	51 018	51 638	51 105	57 803	58 913	60 864	66 000	62 494	67 219
Government consumption	5 341	5 845	5 783	5 830	6 297	6 579	6 828	7 199	6 947	7 410
Gross fixed capital investment	12 742	18 491	18 299	18 701	21 670	21 935	22 882	28 574	24 026	26 028
Construction	8 778	11 727	11 688	12 331	12 543	12 289	12 830	14 037	13 968	13 402
Non-housing	4 814	5 392	4 528	5 037	5 336	5 206	5 354	5 621	5 397	4 913
Housing	3 964	6 335	7 160	7 294	7 207	7 083	7 476	8 416	8 571	8 489
Machinery and equipment	3 964	6 764	6 611	6 370	9 127	9 646	10 052	14 537	10 058	12 626
Increase in stocks	563	687	–693	520	1 513	–939	402	1 486	–2 925	1 371
Total domestic demand	69 825	76 041	75 027	76 156	87 283	86 488	90 976	103 259	90 542	102 028
Exports of goods and services	9 212	11 642	13 786	13 751	14 102	14 627	16 236	17 484	20 138	21 496
Imports of goods and services	10 788	13 267	12 670	13 543	18 014	17 074	18 938	25 715	20 090	26 122
Statistical discrepancy	0	306	163	134	208	312	1 127	1 563	730	621
Gross domestic product	68 249	74 722	76 306	76 498	83 579	84 353	89 401	96 591	91 320	98 023

Source: State Institute of Statistics, *Gross National Product*, and OECD, *National Accounts*.

Table C. **Gross domestic product by kind of activity**

TL billion

	1987	1988	1989	1990	1991	1992	1993	1994	1995
	Current prices								
Agriculture, forestry, fishing	13 314	22 303	37 704	68 692	96 074	163 827	305 525	598 169	1 134 566
Mining	1 475	2 357	4 625	6 269	9 762	14 946	21 814	54 099	98 545
Manufacturing	16 319	29 664	52 561	86 307	139 709	236 573	412 408	853 488	1 751 681
Electricity, gas and water	1 482	2 829	4 408	7 745	13 839	28 602	51 450	112 181	192 169
Construction	5 452	9 998	15 904	24 746	44 139	74 509	145 834	263 720	426 215
Wholesale and retail trade, restaurants and hotels	14 850	25 699	42 653	74 912	117 433	202 369	368 385	760 919	1 550 148
Transport, storage and communication	8 660	15 245	26 317	46 490	74 561	133 338	236 860	514 110	970 932
Financial institutions	6 672	10 137	14 889	25 878	49 287	84 708	152 631	242 929	503 726
Community, social and personal services	1 736	3 198	7 544	14 415	23 006	39 577	71 449	142 795	278 628
Producers of government services	3 789	6 363	15 535	32 525	61 051	111 841	203 922	344 530	619 785
Private non-profit institutions	319	535	891	1 521	2 332	3 553	6 015	9 070	14 577
Imputed bank service change	1 997	3 349	2 562	9 838	23 282	41 188	75 654	163 471	270 344
Import duties	2 652	4 246	6 854	13 397	22 206	40 713	81 229	135 892	284 130
Gross domestic product at factor cost	74 722	129 225	227 324	393 060	630 117	1 093 368	1 981 867	3 868 429	7 554 758
	Percentage volume change, 1987 prices								
Agriculture, forestry, fishing	0.4	7.8	–7.6	6.8	–0.9	4.3	–1.3	–0.7	2.6
Mining	2.5	–4.6	13.0	–2.5	4.5	0.3	–6.4	8.0	–6.9
Manufacturing	10.1	1.6	3.0	9.7	2.4	5.8	9.3	–7.6	13.9
Electricity, gas and water	5.8	10.4	13.9	8.6	4.5	11.8	8.9	3.4	9.6
Construction	14.9	–5.4	6.1	–1.1	1.1	6.2	7.9	–2.0	–4.7
Wholesale and retail trade, restaurants and hotels	19.0	3.5	–2.3	12.3	–0.7	6.9	11.6	–7.6	11.6
Transport, storage and communication	10.2	1.2	3.2	11.9	–0.4	8.1	10.8	–2.0	5.9
Financial institutions	3.6	1.6	2.6	2.3	1.8	0.9	1.7	1.4	2.4
Community, social and personal services	9.1	2.3	0.3	8.1	0.9	5.5	6.9	–4.3	7.5
Producers of government services	–0.2	1.9	1.2	2.9	2.4	3.4	1.8	0.8	2.5
Private non-profit institutions	12.6	1.9	1.8	10.3	3.5	2.2	3.0	–2.5	–1.3
Imputed bank service change	3.8	4.1	2.1	1.9	0.2	–2.3	–0.6	–1.8	0.1
Import duties	28.2	–10.3	–2.6	48.3	4.1	11.3	32.8	–35.2	11.8
Gross domestic product at factor cost	9.5	2.1	0.3	9.3	0.9	6.0	8.0	–5.5	7.3

Source: State Institute of Statistics, *Gross National Product,* and OECD, *National Accounts.*

Table D. **Industrial production**

Percentage changes from a year earlier
Index 1992 = 100

	1991	1992	1993	1994	1995	1995			1996
						II	III	IV	I
Total industry	**3.1**	**5.3**	**5.9**	**–6.2**	**8.6**	**17.2**	**12.7**	**9.5**	**9.1**
Mining	**7.7**	**–2.3**	**–9.3**	**9.3**	**0.1**	**–5.4**	**0.7**	**5.5**	**3.9**
Energy	**21.5**	**–4.9**	**–9.4**	**–5.3**	**–4.7**	**–6.2**	**–5.1**	**–0.3**	**14.9**
Manufacturing	**2.6**	**4.5**	**6.4**	**–8.6**	**9.0**	**19.3**	**13.7**	**9.7**	**8.5**
By manufacturing sector									
Foods, beverages, tobacco	9.4	4.6	1.1	–1.5	2.2	22.7	8.4	–0.6	..
Textile, clothing, leather	–7.0	1.1	0.4	–6.7	0.9	4.9	4.2	3.4	..
Paper and printing	–19.8	17.8	–18.2	14.8	16.6	35.2	15.6	–18.0	..
Chemicals, petroleum	–2.0	2.6	9.2	–1.0	8.9	13.9	8.9	11.2	..
Non-metallic mineral products	3.9	8.0	7.0	–4.9	10.7	18.3	10.2	14.0	..
Basic metal industry	–0.9	6.2	8.9	2.8	0.5	9.9	–3.1	–17.4	..
Machinery and transport equipment	15.3	6.0	14.2	–31.7	24.7	44.3	51.6	41.3	..

Source: State Institute of Statistics, *Turkish Economy and Analysis* and *Monthly Production Index.*

Table E. **Prices**[1]

Annual percentage changes

	Wholesale prices							Consumer prices	
	General index			Agriculture	Mining	Manufacturing industry	Energy	General	Food
	Total	Public	Private						
	Base year 1987 = 100								
Old series									
(1987 weights)	(100)	(27.74)	(72.26)	(23.03)	(2.54)	(69.80)	(4.62)	(100)	(32.10)
1988	70.5	70.3	70.5	44.1	64.1	81.5	40.9	73.7	83.2
1989	64.0	64.2	63.9	71.7	65.0	61.6	69.2	63.2	69.3
1990	52.3	56.7	50.6	70.6	48.7	46.9	56.5	60.3	64.3
1991	55.3	61.3	53.0	50.8	63.2	55.3	75.1	66.0	67.1
1992	62.1	65.2	60.8	62.7	61.6	55.3	97.7	70.1	71.3
1993	58.4	54.5	60.1	62.2	56.7	56.6	67.8	66.1	63.5
1994	120.7	122.5	119.9	97.8	132.8	129.4	102.3	106.3	110.0
1995	88.5	77.0	93.4	118.7	76.6	83.4	47.8	93.6	97.3
	Base year 1994 = 100								
New series									
(1994 weights)	(100)	(23.17)	(76.83)	(22.22)	(2.47)	(71.12)	(4.19)	(100)	(31.09)
1995	86.0			107.8	85.6	81.0	56.4	88.0	92.3
1996 1	64.9			80.1	84.7	59.5	62.5	78.1	69.5
2	63.0			75.1	74.3	57.2	81.8	77.5	65.1
3	65.3	67.6	64.7	72.6	70.1	61.2	85.2	79.3	71.8
4	69.9			74.7	78.4	66.3	96.1	80.8	74.6
5	73.7			83.1	79.4	68.7	96.0	82.9	80.3
6	76.2	77.4	75.9	90.3	87.0	69.5	102.8	82.9	77.6

1. In January 1996, the State Institute of Statistics introduced new weights for both wholesale and consumer prices indices, and shifted the base year from 1987 to 1994.

Source: State Institute of Statistics, *Wholesale and Consumer Price Indices Monthly Bulletin.*

Table F. **Imports by commodities**

$ million

	1985	1986	1987	1988	1989	1990	1991	1992	1993	1994
SITC classification										
0. Food and live animals	289	261	369	180	697	1 179	466	594	839	465
1. Beverages and tobacco	58	125	192	189	225	346	381	330	336	153
2. Crude materials, inedible, except fuels	642	834	1 322	1 353	1 602	1 680	1 614	1 872	2 489	2 272
3. Mineral fuels, lubricants and related materials	3 786	2 192	3 172	3 062	3 258	4 641	3 773	3 782	3 990	3 838
4. Animal and vegetable oils, fats and waxes	215	141	145	227	307	297	393	375	403	454
5. Chemicals and related products, n.e.s.	1 473	1 585	2 146	2 215	2 321	2 830	2 852	3 092	3 527	3 186
6. Manufactured goods classified chiefly by material	1 508	1 512	2 341	2 436	2 795	3 372	3 295	3 606	5 026	4 065
7. Machinery and transport equipment	3 055	4 035	4 054	4 234	4 095	7 030	7 168	8 043	11 228	7 658
8. Miscellanous manufactured articles	249	327	421	442	485	905	990	1 105	1 461	1 091
9. Commodities and transactions not classified elsewhere	0	9	1	2	4	22	114	73	131	87
Total	11 275	11 020	14 163	14 340	15 789	22 302	21 047	22 871	29 429	23 270

Source: OECD, *Foreign Trade by Commodities,* Series C.

Table G. **Exports by commodities**

$ million

	1985	1986	1987	1988	1989	1990	1991	1992	1993	1994
SITC classification										
0. Food and live animals	1 594	1 864	2 163	2 484	2 015	2 302	2 728	2 760	2 794	3 298
1. Beverages and tobacco	337	278	324	278	493	455	593	356	466	471
2. Crude materials, inedible, except fuels	619	604	517	777	837	750	681	503	555	605
3. Mineral fuels, lubricants and related materials	377	185	238	335	260	298	292	235	178	246
4. Animal and vegetable oils, fats and waxes	68	80	83	86	153	139	197	215	187	182
5. Chemicals and related products, n.e.s.	298	410	675	950	936	745	603	629	609	730
6. Manufactured goods classified chiefly by material	2 617	2 206	2 669	3 503	3 391	3 841	3 717	4 155	4 485	5 684
7. Machinery and transport equipment	645	415	1 085	748	587	853	1 016	1 290	1 292	1 720
8. Miscellanous manufactured articles	1 387	1 400	2 411	2 497	2 949	3 567	3 758	4 561	4 775	5 160
9. Commodities and transactions not classified elsewhere	15	15	24	4	7	7	8	10	9	9
Total	7 958	7 457	10 190	11 662	11 627	12 957	13 593	14 715	15 349	18 105

Source: OECD, *Foreign Trade by Commodities,* Series C.

Table H. **Geographic distribution of foreign trade**

$ million

	Imports						Exports					
	1990	1991	1992	1993	1994	1995	1990	1991	1992	1993	1994	1995
OECD countries	14 384	14 230	15 535	20 310	15 485	23 772	8 855	8 904	9 384	9 178	10 940	13 455
EU countries	9 924	9 897	10 657	13 874	10 916	16 862	7 188	7 347	7 934	7 603	8 689	11 077
of which:												
France	1 340	1 227	1 351	1 952	1 458	1 996	737	689	809	771	855	1 033
Germany	3 523	3 232	3 754	4 533	3 646	5 548	3 076	3 413	3 660	3 654	3 969	5 034
Italy	1 727	1 845	1 919	2 558	2 008	3 193	1 106	972	943	750	1 035	1 456
United Kingdom	1 014	1 166	1 187	1 546	1 170	1 830	744	676	796	835	893	1 134
Other OECD countries	4 459	4 332	4 879	6 436	4 569	6 909	1 667	1 557	1 450	1 575	2 251	2 378
of which:												
Japan	1 120	1 092	1 113	1 621	968	1 400	239	226	162	158	187	180
Switzerland	537	489	688	651	473	816	293	246	223	216	240	238
United States	2 282	2 255	2 601	3 351	2 429	3 724	968	913	865	986	1 534	1 513
Central and eastern European countries	1 837	1 742	1 997	725	567	962	798	1 019	1 190	564	656	901
Middle East and North Africa	3 659	2 981	3 238	3 240	3 191	3 857	2 452	2 694	2 763	2 743	2 989	3 234
of which:												
Iran	492	91	365	667	692	689	495	487	455	290	250	266
Iraq	1 047	0	1	0	0	0	215	122	212	160	141	119
Kuwait	54	0	68	84	77	97	92	16	66	104	128	119
Libya	487	281	445	131	320	385	221	237	247	246	180	238
Saudi Arabia	724	1 829	1 665	1 500	1 229	1 383	338	485	486	652	611	467
Other countries	2 423	2 095	2 101	5 155	4 028	7 116	853	977	1 377	2 864	3 521	3 987
Total	22 302	21 047	22 871	29 429	23 270	35 708	12 957	13 593	14 715	15 349	18 105	21 576

Source: OECD, *Monthly Statistics of Foreign Trade*, Series A.

Table I. **Balance of payments**

$ million

	1987	1988	1989	1990	1991	1992	1993	1994	1995
Exports	10 322	11 929	11 780	13 026	13 667	14 891	15 611	18 390	21 975
Imports	13 551	13 706	15 999	22 581	21 007	23 081	29 771	22 606	35 187
Trade balance	–3 229	–1 777	–4 219	–9 555	–7 340	–8 190	–14 160	–4 216	–13 212
Services	33	1 214	1 622	2 437	2 499	3 157	4 014	3 755	6 377
Balance of goods and services	–3 196	–563	–2 597	–7 118	–4 849	–5 033	–10 201	–461	–6 835
Private transfers, net	2 066	1 827	3 135	3 349	2 854	3 147	3 035	2 709	3 425
Official transfers, net	324	332	423	1 144	2 245	912	733	383	1 071
Current balance	–806	1 596	961	–2 625	250	–974	–6 433	2 631	–2 339
Long-term capital	1 841	1 323	1 364	1 037	623	2 252	5 909	933	2 417
Private, net	1 388	2 037	2 456	1 847	1 562	3 351	6 839	2 394	2 954
Official, net	453	–714	–1 092	–810	–939	–1 099	–930	–1 461	–537
Basic balance	1 035	2 919	2 325	–1 588	873	1 278	–524	3 564	78
Non-monetary short-term private capital, net	–542	–351	23	1 362	37	1 641	1 850	–947	2 117
Non-monetary short-term official capital, net	305	–895	–526	359	–322	136	133	. .	. .
Errors and omissions	–506	515	971	–468	948	–1 190	–2 222	1 769	2 275
Balance on non-monetary transactions	292	2 188	2 793	–335	1 536	1 865	–763	4 386	4 470
Private monetary institutions short-term capital	287	–1 035	–81	1 279	–2 735	–381	1 071	–4 180	188
Assets	–434	–1 046	–370	–769	–2 595	–2 474	–3 231	2 591	–1 512
Liabilities	721	11	289	2 048	–140	2 093	4 302	–6 771	1 700
Net transactions of monetary authorities	579	1 153	2 712	944	–1 199	1 484	308	206	4 658
Use of IMF credit	–443	–432	–238	–48	0	0	0	340	347
Miscellaneous official accounts	1	1	–3	–1	2	0	0	0	0
Allocation of SDR's	0	0	0	0	0	0	0	0	0
Change in reserves	137	722	2 471	895	–1 197	1 484	308	546	5 005
Gold	0	0	–14	114	25	0	–6	–79	–27
Currency assets	137	721	2 485	781	–1 223	1 484	314	625	5 032
Reserve position in IMF	0	0	0	0	0	0	0	0	0
Special drawing rights	0	1	0	0	1	0	0	0	0

Source: OECD.

Table J. **External trade indicators**

	Exchange rate TL per $	Effective exchange rate	Terms of trade	Goods and services	
				Exports	Imports
		1987 = 100		1987 prices, TL billion	
1980	76.0	977.1	101.9	3 184	7 024
1981	110.2	803.3	101.8	5 205	7 902
1982	160.7	610.2	101.8	6 976	8 554
1983	223.7	473.3	101.8	7 891	10 002
1984	363.5	319.4	101.8	9 898	11 975
1985	519.6	231.8	101.8	9 707	11 183
1986	669.0	145.6	101.8	9 212	10 788
1987	854.6	100.0	100.0	11 642	13 267
1988	1 419.4	59.1	97.7	13 786	12 670
1989	2 120.0	41.0	89.7	13 751	13 543
1990	2 606.5	30.2	96.6	14 102	18 014
1991	4 168.9	19.5	97.1	14 627	17 074
1992	6 860.6	11.4	96.8	16 236	18 938
1993	10 965.6	7.7	104.0	17 484	25 715
1994	29 778.2	3.0	104.6	20 138	20 090
1995	45 738.4	1.7	98.6	21 496	26 122
1995 Q3	46 298.4	1.6	100.2	21 326	26 819
Q4	52 945.7	1.4	108.1	21 201	30 068
1996 Q1	64 317.2	1.2	. .	. .	. .
Q2	76 387.3	1.0	. .	. .	. .

Source: OECD, *National Accounts* and *Main Economic Indicators.*

Table K. **External debt of Turkey**[1]

Disbursed debt – End of period
$ million

	1986	1987	1988	1989	1990	1991	1992	1993	1994	1995
Medium- and long-term debt	25 752	32 605	34 305	36 006	39 536	41 372	42 932	48 823	54 291	57 577
Multilateral organisations	7 839	9 802	9 192	8 740	9 564	10 069	9 160	8 674	9 183	9 081
IMF	1 085	770	299	48	0	0	0	0	344	573
World Bank, IDA, IFC	4 917	6 550	6 421	6 137	6 435	6 540	5 761	5 440	5 380	5 191
European Investment Bank	571	675	583	561	604	602	463	250	264	86
European Resettlement Fund	1 216	1 757	1 836	1 918	2 439	2 859	2 880	2 952	3 065	3 114
Islamic Development Bank	12	15	22	51	68	54	40	15	117	108
OPEC Fund	30	25	20	15	10	5	3	2	0	0
International Fund for Agricultural Development	8	10	11	10	8	9	13	15	13	9
Bilateral credits	9 646	11 680	11 382	11 431	12 984	14 587	15 035	18 153	20 678	21 558
OECD countries	8 049	10 086	10 038	9 992	11 652	13 169	13 542	16 607	19 001	19 552
OPEC countries	1 013	1 066	886	697	564	438	363	317	236	247
Other countries	584	528	458	742	768	980	1 130	1 229	1 441	1 759
Commercial banks	4 969	6 391	8 891	10 269	10 721	10 992	12 956	15 706	16 113	16 532
Private lenders	3 298	4 732	4 840	5 566	6 267	5 724	5 781	6 290	8 317	10 406
Dresdner Bank scheme	3 069	4 569	4 723	5 500	6 255	5 713	5 771	6 282	8 308	10 397
Short-term debt	6 349	7 623	6 417	5 745	9 500	9 117	12 660	18 533	11 310	15 701
Commercial banks	2 673	3 725	2 950	1 841	3 845	4 144	6 490	9 526	2 901	4 263
Private lenders	3 676	3 898	3 467	3 904	5 655	4 973	6 170	9 007	8 409	11 438
Foreign exchange deposits	1 986	2 619	2 433	2 795	3 976	2 982	2 594	3 097	3 266	4 471
Total debt	32 101	40 228	40 722	41 751	49 036	50 489	55 592	67 356	65 601	73 278
Memorandum items (per cent):										
Total debt/GDP	42.0	46.1	44.8	39.0	32.5	33.4	35.0	37.3	50.4	44.3
Medium- and long-term debt/GDP	33.7	37.4	37.7	33.6	26.2	27.4	27.0	27.1	41.7	34.8
Short-term debt/GDP	8.3	8.7	7.1	5.4	6.3	6.0	8.0	10.3	8.7	9.5
Short-term debt/total debt	19.8	18.9	15.8	13.8	19.4	18.1	22.8	27.5	17.2	21.4
Total debt/foreign exchange revenues	255.8	242.3	205.7	189.4	193.6	195.3	195.4	221.3	200.1	176.6
Total debt by borrower										
General government	51.3	52.3	56.8	57.3	52.2	54.3	51.2	45.7	51.9	47.3
SEEs	9.2	9.2	9.8	9.9	12.6	10.2	9.2	8.1	8.4	6.6
Central Bank	23.7	23.9	20.6	18.9	16.6	14.0	12.1	10.8	14.4	15.7
Private sector	15.8	14.6	12.8	13.9	18.6	21.5	27.5	35.4	25.3	30.5

1. The Turkish authorities have issued a new series of external debt statistics, starting from 1984. Revised series reflect the adjustment for valuation changes in World Bank loans arising from the World Bank's currency pool system and the reclassification of the Dresdner Bank accounts according to maturities. Foreign Military Sales (FMS) refinancing credits are also included. In 1988, $1 503 million and in 1989 $403 million FMS loans were rescheduled by a group of US bank under US Treasury guarantee. Other military debt is excluded.

Source: Data provided by the Undersecretariat of the Treasury and the Foreign Trade, and Central Bank of Turkey.

Table L. **Money and banking**

TL billion, end of period

	1988	1989	1990	1991	1992	1993	1994	1995
Money supply								
Notes and coins	3 426	6 840	11 378	17 449	30 389	51 645	102 328	189 542
Sight deposits	7 886	12 718	20 020	29 344	47 952	77 442	128 519	206 505
M1	11 312	19 558	31 398	46 793	78 341	129 087	230 847	396 047
Time deposits	15 883	27 582	40 172	70 325	112 395	153 355	399 501	874 376
M2	27 194	47 139	71 570	117 118	190 736	282 442	630 348	1 270 423
Foreign exchange deposits	9 512	14 135	21 793	50 936	103 234	190 617	565 005	1 355 094
M2Y	36 707	61 274	93 363	168 054	293 970	473 059	1 195 353	2 625 517
Central Bank								
Total assets	38 362	48 988	60 987	96 789	177 244	285 801	693 005	1 421 112
Foreign assets	11 429	17 948	25 583	38 736	75 758	128 126	368 701	911 817
Domestic assets	26 933	31 040	35 404	58 053	101 486	157 675	324 304	509 295
Cash credits	10 039	10 892	10 644	28 199	72 044	127 344	226 488	478 750
Credit to public sector	7 020	7 860	5 324	22 904	62 602	108 482	214 161	466 496
Credit to private sector	3 019	3 032	5 320	5 295	9 442	18 862	12 327	12 254
Other items	–287	–1 058	–1 648	–2 575	–5 293	–1 593	–35 989	–14 467
Devaluation account	17 181	21 206	26 408	32 429	34 735	31 924	133 805	45 012
Total liabilities	38 362	48 988	60 987	96 789	177 244	285 801	693 005	1 421 112
Reserve money	10 143	17 035	23 871	37 244	61 195	101 721	185 738	343 484
Monetary base	11 349	17 365	22 944	42 828	82 974	123 556	186 876	359 410
Central bank money	11 852	18 528	23 837	43 993	87 837	128 113	193 140	372 794
Foreign currency liabilities	26 511	30 460	37 150	52 796	89 407	157 688	499 865	1 048 318
Deposit money banks								
Deposits[1]	38 013	61 648	93 931	164 669	296 151	522 500	1 203 149	
Credits	23 871	39 357	69 287	106 491	195 182	363 026	630 583	
Total bank credits (net of Central Bank advances to banks)	29 012	43 580	74 659	130 796	244 420	453 771	773 943	
Central bank	3 509	3 506	4 449	18 454	42 584	82 936	148 208	
Deposit money banks	22 769	36 522	65 198	101 452	185 419	342 182	575 107	
Investment banks	2 734	3 552	5 012	10 890	16 418	28 653	50 629	

1. Including interbank and foreign currency deposits.

Source: Central Bank of Turkey, *Quarterly Bulletin.*

Table M. **Public sector borrowing**

	1988	1989	1990	1991	1992	1993	1994	1995
Public sector deficit (TL billion)	–6 235	–12 283	–29 324	–64 469	–116 582	–244 570	–314 254	–494 959
General government	–3 430	–7 863	–14 338	–44 526	–80 269	–195 645	–259 384	–452 004
State economic enterprises (SEEs)	–2 805	–4 420	–14 986	–19 943	–36 313	–48 925	–54 870	–42 955
Public sector deficit/GDP	–4.8	–5.3	–7.4	–10.2	–10.6	–12.2	–8.1	–6.5
General government	–2.7	–3.4	–3.6	–7.0	–7.3	–9.8	–6.7	–5.9
Central government	–3.0	–3.3	–3.0	–5.3	–4.3	–6.7	–3.9	–4.2
Local administrations	–0.4	–0.2	0.0	–0.3	–0.8	–1.0	–0.6	–0.5
Revolving funds	0.2	0.4	0.3	0.0	0.0	0.0	0.0	0.0
Extra-budgetary funds [1]	0.5	–0.2	–0.9	–1.5	–2.2	–2.1	–2.2	–1.2
SEEs [2]	–2.2	–1.9	–3.8	–3.1	–3.3	–2.4	–1.4	–0.6
Sources of financing (per cent of total)								
Central Bank	0.5	0.2	0.1	1.7	1.6	2.7	1.3	1.2
Foreign borrowing, net [3]	0.2	–0.1	0.0	0.3	0.4	1.0	–1.7	–1.1
Domestic borrowing, net [3]	2.7	3.2	2.6	4.1	5.1	5.3	5.8	4.9
Unidentified	1.4	2.0	4.7	4.1	3.5	3.3	2.7	1.5
Memorandum items:								
Public sector debt/GDP	58.0	50.5	39.6	41.4	42.7	41.7	57.7	48.3
Domestic	22.0	18.4	14.5	15.5	17.8	18.0	20.7	18.0
Foreign	36.0	32.1	25.0	25.9	24.9	23.7	37.1	30.2
SEEs								
Domestic	n.a.	n.a.	n.a.	n.a.	n.a.	n.a.	n.a.	n.a.
Foreign	4.4	4.0	3.1	3.4	3.2	3.0	4.2	2.9

1. Including State economic enterprises in the process of privatisation.
2. Including non-financial SEEs.
3. Consolidated budget.

Source: Undersecretariat of Treasury and Foreign Trade, *1995 External Debt Bulletin* and *Treasury Monthly Indicators.*

Table N. **Central government budget**

TL billion

	1988	1989	1990	1991	1992	1993	1994	1995
Revenue	17 587	31 369	56 573	96 747	174 224	351 392	745 116	1 404 100
Tax revenue	14 232	25 550	45 399	78 643	141 602	264 273	587 760	1 085 400
Non-tax revenue	3 355	5 819	11 174	18 104	32 622	87 119	157 356	318 700
Expenditure	21 447	38 871	68 527	130 263	221 658	485 249	897 296	1 720 700
Current personnel expenditure	5 053	12 539	26 465	49 291	94 076	169 511	273 062	502 700
Other current expenditure	2 407	4 121	6 987	11 112	20 145	35 318	73 407	142 800
Investment	3 564	5 818	10 055	17 146	29 239	53 161	72 788	102 400
Transfers	10 423	16 393	25 020	52 714	78 198	227 259	478 039	972 800
of which:								
SEEs	1 025	1 223	1 265	12 191	8 145	25 850	21 850	45 500
Interest payment	4 978	8 259	13 966	24 073	40 298	116 470	298 284	576 100
Budget balance	–3 860	–7 502	–11 954	–33 516	–47 434	–133 857	–152 180	–316 600
Deferred payments	36	38	1 161	3 555	–778	10 905	20 092	52 100
Advance payments	–117	–677	–1 561	–3 465	–11 227	–3 151	–19 837	–29 700
Cash balance	–3 941	–8 141	–12 354	–33 426	–59 439	–126 103	–151 925	–294 200
Foreign borrowing (net)	176	–404	41	1 921	4 038	21 062	–67 174	85 700
Domestic borrowing (net)	2 433	5 982	7 942	2 279	15 408	30 135	–70 338	–81 300
Short-term borrowing (net)	1 064	1 452	2 263	23 509	41 372	75 251	296 073	291 900
Central Bank	675	457	331	10 719	17 394	53 010	51 857	94 700
Treasury bills	389	995	1 932	12 790	23 978	22 241	244 216	197 200
Other borrowing [1]	268	1 111	2 108	5 718	–1 380	–345	–6 636	–2 100

1. Including errors and omissions and change in cash/bank.

Source: Undersecretariat of Treasury and Foreign Trade, *Treasury Monthly Indicators.*

Table O. **Central government budget revenue**

TL billion

	1987	1988	1989	1990	1991	1992	1993	1994
Taxes on income	4 425	6 919	13 469	23 246	40 419	70 134	125 793	246 921
Taxes on wealth	68	147	177	411	675	1 258	2 531	36 892
Taxes on goods and services	2 768	4 487	7 639	13 667	24 678	47 341	89 447	214 672
Taxes on foreign trade	1 777	2 672	4 245	8 057	12 864	22 849	46 213	89 575
Abolished taxes	13	7	18	18	7	20	289	31
Total tax revenue	9 051	14 232	25 548	45 399	78 643	141 602	264 273	588 091
Non-tax regular revenue	809	1 353	2 439	4 267	3 926	7 649	17 636	49 344
Special revenue and funds	34	1 228	1 950	5 401	13 803	24 899	68 936	106 645
Total non-tax revenue	843	2 581	4 389	9 668	17 729	32 548	86 572	155 989
Annex budget revenue	206	351	440	1 506	2 711	3 920	6 488	9 360
Total consolidated budget revenue	10 100	17 164	30 377	56 573	99 083	178 070	357 333	753 440

Source: Ministry of Finance and Customs; State Institute of Statistics, *Monthly Bulletin of Statistics.*

BASIC STATISTICS

BASIC STATISTICS:

INTERNATIONAL COMPARISONS

	Units	Reference period [1]	Australia	Austria
Population				
Total	Thousands	1994	17 840	8 031
Inhabitants per sq. km	Number	1994	2	96
Net average annual increase over previous 10 years	%	1994	1.4	0.6
Employment				
Total civilian employment (TCE)[2]	Thousands	1994	7 680 (93)	3 737
of which: Agriculture	% of TCE	1994	5.3 (93)	7.2
Industry	% of TCE	1994	23.7 (93)	33.2
Services	% of TCE	1994	71 (93)	59.6
Gross domestic product (GDP)				
At current prices and current exchange rates	Bill. US$	1994	331.6	198.1
Per capita	US$	1994	18 588	24 670
At current prices using current PPP's[3]	Bill. US$	1994	327.9	162.3
Per capita	US$	1994	18 382	20 210
Average annual volume growth over previous 5 years	%	1994	2.2	2.5
Gross fixed capital formation (GFCF)	% of GDP	1994	21.4	24.8
of which: Machinery and equipment	% of GDP	1993	9.8	8.7
Residential construction	% of GDP	1993	5.2	6.3
Average annual volume growth over previous 5 years	%	1994	0.8	3.7
Gross saving ratio[4]	% of GDP	1994	16.8	25.[illegible]
General government				
Current expenditure on goods and services	% of GDP	1994	17.5	
Current disbursements[5]	% of GDP	1993	36.9	48.4
Current receipts	% of GDP	1993	33.5	48.[illegible]
Net official development assistance	% of GNP	1993	0.34	0.3[illegible]
Indicators of living standards				
Private consumption per capita using current PPP's[3]	US$	1993	10 803	10 54[illegible]
Passenger cars, per 1 000 inhabitants	Number	1990	430	38[illegible]
Telephones, per 1 000 inhabitants	Number	1991	464	43[illegible]
Television sets, per 1 000 inhabitants	Number	1991	480	47[illegible]
Doctors, per 1 000 inhabitants	Number	1993	2.2 (91)	2.[illegible]
Infant mortality per 1 000 live births	Number		6.1	6.[illegible]
Wages and prices (average annual increase over previous 5 years)				
Wages (earnings or rates according to availability)	%	1994	3	5.[illegible]
Consumer prices	%	1994	3	3.[illegible]
Foreign trade				
Exports of goods, fob*	Mill. US$	1994	47 363	44 88[illegible]
As % of GDP	%	1994	14.3	22.[illegible]
Average annual increase over previous 5 years	%	1994	5	6.[illegible]
Imports of goods, cif*	Mill. US$	1994	49 731	55 07[illegible]
As % of GDP	%	1994	15	27.[illegible]
Average annual increase over previous 5 years	%	1994	4	7.[illegible]
Total official reserves[6]	Mill. SDRs	1994	7 730	11 52[illegible]
As ratio of average monthly imports of goods	Ratio	1994	1.9	2.[illegible]

* At current prices and exchange rates.

1. Unless otherwise stated.
2. According to the definitions used in OECD *Labour Force Statistics.*
3. PPPs = Purchasing Power Parities.
4. Gross saving = Gross national disposable income minus private and government consumption.
5. Current disbursements = Current expenditure on goods and services plus current transfers and payments of property income.
6. Gold included in reserves is valued at 35 SDRs per ounce. End of year.

BASIC STATISTICS: INTERNATIONAL COMPARISONS

gium	Canada	Denmark	Finland	France	Germany	Greece	Iceland	Ireland	Italy	Japan	Luxembourg	Mexico	Netherlands	New Zealand	Norway	Portugal	Spain	Sweden	Switzerland	Turkey	United Kingdom	United States
124	29 251	5 206	5 088	57 960	81 407	10 430	267	3 571	57 190	124 960	398	93 010	15 382	3 526	4 337	9 900	39 150	8 781	6 994	60 573	58 375	260 651
332	3	121	15	106	228	79	3	51	190	331	153	47	377	13	13	107	78	20	169	78	238	28
0.3	1.6	0.2	0.4	0.5	2.9	0.5	1.1	0.1	0	0.4	0.8	2	0.6	0.8	0.5	–0.1	0.2	0.5	0.7	2.1	0.3	1
724 (92)	13 292	2 508	2 015	21 781 (93)	35 894	3 790	138	1 168 (93)	20 152 (93)	64 530	162 (91)	32 439	6 631	1 560	1970 (93)	4 372	11 760	3 926	3 772	19 664	25 044 (93)	123 060
2.6 (92)	4.1	5.1	8.3	5.1 (93)	3.3	20.8	9.4	12.7 (93)	7.5 (93)	5.8	3.7 (91)	25.8	4	10.4	5.6 (93)	11.5	9.8	3.4	4	44.8	2.2 (93)	2.9
27.7 (92)	22.6	26.8	26.8	27.7 (93)	37.6	23.6	26.1	27.7 (93)	33 (93)	34	31.5 (91)	22.2	23	25	23.1 (93)	32.8	30.1	25	28.8	22.2	26.2 (93)	24
9.7 (92)	73.3	68.1	64.9	67.2 (93)	59.1	55.5	65.2	59.7 (93)	59.6 (93)	60.2	64.8 (91)	52.1	73	64.6	71.3 (93)	55.7	60.2	71.6	67.2	33	71.6 (93)	73.1
7.9	544	146.7	97.2	1 328.5	1 832.3[8]	73.1 (93)	6.2	52	1 017.8	4 590	10.6 (92)	371.2	334.3	51.2	103.4 (93)	87	482.4	196.6	257.3	130.7	1 019.5	6 649.8
515	18 598	28 181	19 106	22 944	27 826[8]	7 051 (93)	23 199	14 550	17 796	36 732	27 073 (92)	3 991	21 733	14 513	23 984 (93)	8 792	12 321	22 389	36 790	2 157	17 468	25 512
4.2	596.7	107	82.5	1 111.8	1 601.7[8]	118	5.1	54.3	1 068.4	2 593.7	11.7	673.3	285.9	57.3	95.3	122	531.7	153	167.4	319.3	1 030.2	6 649.8
166	20 401	20 546	16 208	19 201	24 325[8]	1 450	19 271	15 212	18 681	20 756	29 454	7 239	18 589	16 248	21 968	12 335	13 581	17 422	23 942	5 271	17 650	25 512
1.6	1.1	1.9	–1.6	1.1	2.6[8]	1.4 (93)	0.6	4.7	1	2.1	4.1 (92)	3	2.3	2.5	2.1 (93)	1.4	1.5	–0.3	0.5	3.6	0.8	2.1
7.4	18.7	14.8	14.3	18.1	18.5	17.4 (93)	15.2	15.1	16.4	28.6	20.4 (93)	20.7	19.3	20	22 (93)	25.7	19.8	13.7	22.8	24.5	15	17.2
7.8	6.2	7.2	5.90	8.10	7.5	7.8	3.9	6.3	7.4	11.5	..	9.4	8.6	9.3	..	..	5.7	5.7	7.5	10.3	7.3	7.7
4.6	6.1	2.9	3.7	4.9	6.5	3.6	4.4	4.1	5.3	5.4	..	4.9	5.1	4.9	..	..	4.1	4	14.9[10]	9.1	3.1	4
0.4	–0.1	–2.8	–12.9	–1	0.8	2.7 (93)	–4	1	–2.3	1.4	6.5 (92)	7.7	0.4	5.8	–3.93	2.7	–1.2	–7.6	–0.4	5.1	–2.1	4.6
22	16	17	16.6	19	21	15.5 (93)	16.9	19.5	18.8	31.2	60.2 (92)	15.1	24.4	20.7	21.9 (93)	24.2	18.8	13.7	29.3	22.5	13.5	16.2
15	20.2	25.3	22.4	19.6	17.7	19.1 (93)	20.6	16	17.1	9.8	17.1 (92)	11.8[9]	14.2	14.7	22.1 (93)	17.2	16.9	27.3	14.1	11.7	21.6	16.4
5.3	49	61.1	58.9	51.5	45.6	51.2	34.9	..	53.2	26.9	..	..	55.4	..	..	..	43.7	67.3	36.7	..	42.7	35.8
0.1	43	58.3	52.5	46.8	45.7	40.2	35.9	..	47.1	32.9	..	..	54.5	..	..	..	40.1	59	36	..	36.8	31.7
.41	0.46	1.03	0.76	0.66	0.44	..	..	0.15	0.42	0.27	0.34 (92)	..	0.88	0.22	1.23	0.36	0.32	1.33	0.49	..	0.34	0.19
90	11 863	10 042	8 814	11 395	10 733	6 367	11 546	7 750	11 029	11 791	15 545	4 853	10 726	9 266	9 826	7 780	8 412	9 240	13 730	3 617	10 942	16 444
387	469	311	386	413	480[8]	169	464	228	478	282	470	85	356	440	378	260	307	418	441	29	361	568
410	586	577	544	511	420[8]	413	527	300	400	454	511	70	477	436	515	273	340	687	603	143	445	553
451	639	536	501	407	556[8]	197	319	276	421	613	267	148	485	443	423	187	400	468	406	175	434	814
3.7	2.2	2.8 (92)	2.6 (92)	2.8	3.2 (92)	3.8 (92)	3	1.7 (92)	1.7 (91)	1.7 (92)	2.1 (92)	1	2.5 (90)	2	3.2 (92)	2.9	4.1	3	3	0.9	1.5 (92)	2.3 (92)
8	6.8	5.4	4.4	6.5	5.8	8.5	4.8	5.9	7.3	4.5 (92)	8.5 (92)	18	6.3	7.3	5	8.7	7.6	4.8	5.6	52.6	6.6	8.5 (92)
3.7	3.3	3.5	4.8	3.5	5.2	14.6	..	4.6	5.9	2.4	..	5.3	3.2	2.1	4	..	7.2	5.4	..	..	6.7	2.8
2.8	2.8	2.1	3.3	2.5	3.3	16.2	6.3	2.7	5.2	2	3.1	16.1	2.8	2.5	2.7	9	5.6	5.7	3.9	73	4.6	3.6
259[7]	165 358	41 850	29 514	235 337	422 243	8 958	1 628	34 125	189 802	396 149	..	60 882	155 084	12 169	34 645	17 072	73 129	61 122	70 467	18 456	205 170	512 627
0.2	30.4	28.5	30.4	17.7	23	11.5 (93)	26.3	65.7	18.6	8.6	..	16.4	46.4	23.8	30.9 (93)	19.6	15.2	31.1	27.4	14.1	20.1	7.7
6.5	7.1	8.3	4.9	5.6	4.4	3.4	2.7	10.5	6.2	7.6	..	21.7	7.6	6.5	5	6.1	10.5	3.4	6.4	9.5	6.1	7.1
06[7]	148 297	35 932	23 091	220 508	376 566	21 111	1 464	25 812	167 690	274 916	..	79 346	139 800	11 859	27 345	25 967	92 182	51 730	68 126	22 976	227 026	663 256
5.3	27.3	24.5	23.8	16.6	20.6	30.1 (93)	23.6	49.7	16.5	6	..	21.4	41.8	23.2	23.3 (93)	29.9	19.1	26.3	26.5	17.6	22.3	10
5	5.4	6.1	–1.3	3.5	6.9	5.4	0.7	8.1	1.9	5.5	..	25.5	6.1	6.1	2.9	6.6	5.2	1	3.2	37.9	2.8	7
505[7]	8 416	6 203	7 304	17 986	52 994	9 924	201	4 189	22 102	86 214	..	4 301	23 655	2 540	13 033	10 627	28 475	15 929	23 790	4 911	28 094	43 350
0.9	0.7	2.1	3.8	1	1.7	5.6	1.6	1.9	1.6	3.8	..	0.7	2	2.6	5.7	4.9	3.7	3.7	4.2	2.6	1.5	0.8

November 1995

Data refer to the Belgo-Luxembourg Economic Union.
Data refer to western Germany.
Refers to the public sector including public enterprises.
Including non-residential construction.
ces: Population and Employment: OECD, *Labour Force Statistics*. GDP, GFCF, and General Government: OECD, *National Accounts*, Vol. I and *OECD Economic Outlook*, Historical Statistics. Indicators of living standards: Miscellaneous national publications.
Wages and Prices: OECD, *Main Economic Indicators*. Foreign trade: OECD, *Monthly Foreign Trade Statistics*, series A. Total official reserves: IMF, *International Financial Statistics*.

EMPLOYMENT OPPORTUNITIES

Economics Department, OECD

The Economics Department of the OECD offers challenging and rewarding opportunities to economists interested in applied policy analysis in an international environment. The Department's concerns extend across the entire field of economic policy analysis, both macroeconomic and microeconomic. Its main task is to provide, for discussion by committees of senior officials from Member countries, documents and papers dealing with current policy concerns. Within this programme of work, three major responsibilities are:

- to prepare regular surveys of the economies of individual Member countries;
- to issue full twice-yearly reviews of the economic situation and prospects of the OECD countries in the context of world economic trends;
- to analyse specific policy issues in a medium-term context for the OECD as a whole, and to a lesser extent for the non-OECD countries.

The documents prepared for these purposes, together with much of the Department's other economic work, appear in published form in the *OECD Economic Outlook, OECD Economic Surveys, OECD Economic Studies* and the Department's *Working Papers* series.

The Department maintains a world econometric model, INTERLINK, which plays an important role in the preparation of the policy analyses and twice-yearly projections. The availability of extensive cross-country data bases and good computer resources facilitates comparative empirical analysis, much of which is incorporated into the model.

The Department is made up of about 80 professional economists from a variety of backgrounds and Member countries. Most projects are carried out by small teams and last from four to eighteen months. Within the Department, ideas and points of view are widely discussed; there is a lively professional interchange, and all professional staff have the opportunity to contribute actively to the programme of work.

Skills the Economics Department is looking for:

a) Solid competence in using the tools of both microeconomic and macroeconomic theory to answer policy questions. Experience indicates that this normally requires the equivalent of a Ph.D. in economics or substantial relevant professional experience to compensate for a lower degree.

b) Solid knowledge of economic statistics and quantitative methods; this includes how to identify data, estimate structural relationships, apply basic techniques of time series analysis, and test hypotheses. It is essential to be able to interpret results sensibly in an economic policy context.

c) A keen interest in and extensive knowledge of policy issues, economic developments and their political/social contexts.

d) Interest and experience in analysing questions posed by policy-makers and presenting the results to them effectively and judiciously. Thus, work experience in government agencies or policy research institutions is an advantage.

e) The ability to write clearly, effectively, and to the point. The OECD is a bilingual organisation with French and English as the official languages. Candidates must have excellent knowledge of one of these languages, and some knowledge of the other. Knowledge of other languages might also be an advantage for certain posts.

f) For some posts, expertise in a particular area may be important, but a successful candidate is expected to be able to work on a broader range of topics relevant to the work of the Department. Thus, except in rare cases, the Department does not recruit narrow specialists.

g) The Department works on a tight time schedule with strict deadlines. Moreover, much of the work in the Department is carried out in small groups. Thus, the ability to work with other economists from a variety of cultural and professional backgrounds, to supervise junior staff, and to produce work on time is important.

General information

The salary for recruits depends on educational and professional background. Positions carry a basic salary from FF 305 700 or FF 377 208 for Administrators (economists) and from FF 438 348 for Principal Administrators (senior economists). This may be supplemented by expatriation and/or family allowances, depending on nationality, residence and family situation. Initial appointments are for a fixed term of two to three years.

Vacancies are open to candidates from OECD Member countries. The Organisation seeks to maintain an appropriate balance between female and male staff and among nationals from Member countries.

For further information on employment opportunities in the Economics Department, contact:

Administrative Unit
Economics Department
OECD
2, rue André-Pascal
75775 PARIS CEDEX 16
FRANCE

E-Mail: compte.esadmin@oecd.org

Applications citing ''ECSUR'', together with a detailed *curriculum vitae* in English or French, should be sent to the Head of Personnel at the above address.

MAIN SALES OUTLETS OF OECD PUBLICATIONS
PRINCIPAUX POINTS DE VENTE DES PUBLICATIONS DE L'OCDE

AUSTRALIA – AUSTRALIE
D.A. Information Services
648 Whitehorse Road, P.O.B 163
Mitcham, Victoria 3132 Tel. (03) 9210.7777
Fax: (03) 9210.7788

AUSTRIA – AUTRICHE
Gerold & Co.
Graben 31
Wien I Tel. (0222) 533.50.14
Fax: (0222) 512.47.31.29

BELGIUM – BELGIQUE
Jean De Lannoy
Avenue du Roi, Koningslaan 202
B-1060 Bruxelles Tel. (02) 538.51.69/538.08.41
Fax: (02) 538.08.41

CANADA
Renouf Publishing Company Ltd.
1294 Algoma Road
Ottawa, ON K1B 3W8 Tel. (613) 741.4333
Fax: (613) 741.5439

Stores:
61 Sparks Street
Ottawa, ON K1P 5R1 Tel. (613) 238.8985
12 Adelaide Street West
Toronto, ON M5H 1L6 Tel. (416) 363.3171
Fax: (416)363.59.63

Les Éditions La Liberté Inc.
3020 Chemin Sainte-Foy
Sainte-Foy, PQ G1X 3V6 Tel. (418) 658.3763
Fax: (418) 658.3763

Federal Publications Inc.
165 University Avenue, Suite 701
Toronto, ON M5H 3B8 Tel. (416) 860.1611
Fax: (416) 860.1608

Les Publications Fédérales
1185 Université
Montréal, QC H3B 3A7 Tel. (514) 954.1633
Fax: (514) 954.1635

CHINA – CHINE
China National Publications Import
Export Corporation (CNPIEC)
16 Gongti E. Road, Chaoyang District
P.O. Box 88 or 50
Beijing 100704 PR Tel. (01) 506.6688
Fax: (01) 506.3101

CHINESE TAIPEI – TAIPEI CHINOIS
Good Faith Worldwide Int'l. Co. Ltd.
9th Floor, No. 118, Sec. 2
Chung Hsiao E. Road
Taipei Tel. (02) 391.7396/391.7397
Fax: (02) 394.9176

DENMARK – DANEMARK
Munksgaard Book and Subscription Service
35, Nørre Søgade, P.O. Box 2148
DK-1016 København K Tel. (33) 12.85.70
Fax: (33) 12.93.87

J. H. Schultz Information A/S,
Herstedvang 12,
DK – 2620 Albertslung Tel. 43 63 23 00
Fax: 43 63 19 69

Internet: s-info@inet.uni-c.dk

EGYPT – ÉGYPTE
Middle East Observer
41 Sherif Street
Cairo Tel. 392.6919
Fax: 360-6804

FINLAND – FINLANDE
Akateeminen Kirjakauppa
Keskuskatu 1, P.O. Box 128
00100 Helsinki

Subscription Services/Agence d'abonnements :
P.O. Box 23
00371 Helsinki Tel. (358 0) 121 4416
Fax: (358 0) 121.4450

FRANCE
OECD/OCDE
Mail Orders/Commandes par correspondance :
2, rue André-Pascal
75775 Paris Cedex 16 Tel. (33-1) 45.24.82.00
Fax: (33-1) 49.10.42.76
Telex: 640048 OCDE
Internet: Compte.PUBSINQ@oecd.org

Orders via Minitel, France only/
Commandes par Minitel, France exclusivement :
36 15 OCDE

OECD Bookshop/Librairie de l'OCDE :
33, rue Octave-Feuillet
75016 Paris Tél. (33-1) 45.24.81.81
(33-1) 45.24.81.67

Dawson
B.P. 40
91121 Palaiseau Cedex Tel. 69.10.47.00
Fax: 64.54.83.26

Documentation Française
29, quai Voltaire
75007 Paris Tel. 40.15.70.00

Economica
49, rue Héricart
75015 Paris Tel. 45.75.05.67
Fax: 40.58.15.70

Gibert Jeune (Droit-Économie)
6, place Saint-Michel
75006 Paris Tel. 43.25.91.19

Librairie du Commerce International
10, avenue d'Iéna
75016 Paris Tel. 40.73.34.60

Librairie Dunod
Université Paris-Dauphine
Place du Maréchal-de-Lattre-de-Tassigny
75016 Paris Tel. 44.05.40.13

Librairie Lavoisier
11, rue Lavoisier
75008 Paris Tel. 42.65.39.95

Librairie des Sciences Politiques
30, rue Saint-Guillaume
75007 Paris Tel. 45.48.36.02

P.U.F.
49, boulevard Saint-Michel
75005 Paris Tel. 43.25.83.40

Librairie de l'Université
12*a*, rue Nazareth
13100 Aix-en-Provence Tel. (16) 42.26.18.08

Documentation Française
165, rue Garibaldi
69003 Lyon Tel. (16) 78.63.32.23

Librairie Decitre
29, place Bellecour
69002 Lyon Tel. (16) 72.40.54.54

Librairie Sauramps
Le Triangle
34967 Montpellier Cedex 2 Tel. (16) 67.58.85.15
Fax: (16) 67.58.27.36

A la Sorbonne Actual
23, rue de l'Hôtel-des-Postes
06000 Nice Tel. (16) 93.13.77.75
Fax: (16) 93.80.75.69

GERMANY – ALLEMAGNE
OECD Bonn Centre
August-Bebel-Allee 6
D-53175 Bonn Tel. (0228) 959.120
Fax: (0228) 959.12.17

GREECE – GRÈCE
Librairie Kauffmann
Stadiou 28
10564 Athens Tel. (01) 32.55.321
Fax: (01) 32.30.320

HONG-KONG
Swindon Book Co. Ltd.
Astoria Bldg. 3F
34 Ashley Road, Tsimshatsui
Kowloon, Hong Kong Tel. 2376.2062
Fax: 2376.0685

HUNGARY – HONGRIE
Euro Info Service
Margitsziget, Európa Ház
1138 Budapest Tel. (1) 111.62.16
Fax: (1) 111.60.61

ICELAND – ISLANDE
Mál Mog Menning
Laugavegi 18, Pósthólf 392
121 Reykjavik Tel. (1) 552.4240
Fax: (1) 562.3523

INDIA – INDE
Oxford Book and Stationery Co.
Scindia House
New Delhi 110001 Tel. (11) 331.5896/5308
Fax: (11) 332.5993

17 Park Street
Calcutta 700016 Tel. 240832

INDONESIA – INDONÉSIE
Pdii-Lipi
P.O. Box 4298
Jakarta 12042 Tel. (21) 573.34.67
Fax: (21) 573.34.67

IRELAND – IRLANDE
Government Supplies Agency
Publications Section
4/5 Harcourt Road
Dublin 2 Tel. 661.31.11
Fax: 475.27.60

ISRAEL – ISRAËL
Praedicta
5 Shatner Street
P.O. Box 34030
Jerusalem 91430 Tel. (2) 52.84.90/1/2
Fax: (2) 52.84.93

R.O.Y. International
P.O. Box 13056
Tel Aviv 61130 Tel. (3) 546 1423
Fax: (3) 546 1442

Palestinian Authority/Middle East:
INDEX Information Services
P.O.B. 19502
Jerusalem Tel. (2) 27.12.19
Fax: (2) 27.16.34

ITALY – ITALIE
Libreria Commissionaria Sansoni
Via Duca di Calabria 1/1
50125 Firenze Tel. (055) 64.54.15
Fax: (055) 64.12.57

Via Bartolini 29
20155 Milano Tel. (02) 36.50.83

Editrice e Libreria Herder
Piazza Montecitorio 120
00186 Roma Tel. 679.46.28
Fax: 678.47.51

Libreria Hoepli
Via Hoepli 5
20121 Milano Tel. (02) 86.54.46
Fax: (02) 805.28.86

Libreria Scientifica
Dott. Lucio de Biasio 'Aeiou'
Via Coronelli, 6
20146 Milano Tel. (02) 48.95.45.52
Fax: (02) 48.95.45.48

JAPAN – JAPON

OECD Tokyo Centre
Landic Akasaka Building
2-3-4 Akasaka, Minato-ku
Tokyo 107 Tel. (81.3) 3586.2016
Fax: (81.3) 3584.7929

KOREA – CORÉE

Kyobo Book Centre Co. Ltd.
P.O. Box 1658, Kwang Hwa Moon
Seoul Tel. 730.78.91
Fax: 735.00.30

MALAYSIA – MALAISIE

University of Malaya Bookshop
University of Malaya
P.O. Box 1127, Jalan Pantai Baru
59700 Kuala Lumpur
Malaysia Tel. 756.5000/756.5425
Fax: 756.3246

MEXICO – MEXIQUE

OECD Mexico Centre
Edificio INFOTEC
Av. San Fernando no. 37
Col. Toriello Guerra
Tlalpan C.P. 14050
Mexico D.F. Tel. (525) 665 47 99
Fax: (525) 606 13 07

Revistas y Periodicos Internacionales S.A. de C.V.
Florencia 57 - 1004
Mexico, D.F. 06600 Tel. 207.81.00
Fax: 208.39.79

NETHERLANDS – PAYS-BAS

SDU Uitgeverij Plantijnstraat
Externe Fondsen
Postbus 20014
2500 EA's-Gravenhage Tel. (070) 37.89.880
Voor bestellingen: Fax: (070) 34.75.778

NEW ZEALAND – NOUVELLE-ZÉLANDE

GPLegislation Services
P.O. Box 12418
Thorndon, Wellington Tel. (04) 496.5655
Fax: (04) 496.5698

NORWAY – NORVÈGE

NIC INFO A/S
Bertrand Narvesens vei 2
P.O. Box 6512 Etterstad
0606 Oslo 6 Tel. (022) 57.33.00
Fax: (022) 68.19.01

PAKISTAN

Mirza Book Agency
65 Shahrah Quaid-E-Azam
Lahore 54000 Tel. (42) 735.36.01
Fax: (42) 576.37.14

PHILIPPINE – PHILIPPINES

International Booksource Center Inc.
Rm 179/920 Cityland 10 Condo Tower 2
HV dela Costa Ext cor Valero St.
Makati Metro Manila Tel. (632) 817 9676
Fax: (632) 817 1741

POLAND – POLOGNE

Ars Polona
00-950 Warszawa
Krakowskie Przedmieácie 7 Tel. (22) 264760
Fax: (22) 268673

PORTUGAL

Livraria Portugal
Rua do Carmo 70-74
Apart. 2681
1200 Lisboa Tel. (01) 347.49.82/5
Fax: (01) 347.02.64

SINGAPORE – SINGAPOUR

Gower Asia Pacific Pte Ltd.
Golden Wheel Building
41, Kallang Pudding Road, No. 04-03
Singapore 1334 Tel. 741.5166
Fax: 742.9356

SPAIN – ESPAGNE

Mundi-Prensa Libros S.A.
Castelló 37, Apartado 1223
Madrid 28001 Tel. (91) 431.33.99
Fax: (91) 575.39.98

Mundi-Prensa Barcelona
Consell de Cent No. 391
08009 – Barcelona Tel. (93) 488.34.92
Fax: (93) 487.76.59

Llibreria de la Generalitat
Palau Moja
Rambla dels Estudis, 118
08002 – Barcelona
(Subscripcions) Tel. (93) 318.80.12
(Publicacions) Tel. (93) 302.67.23
Fax: (93) 412.18.54

SRI LANKA

Centre for Policy Research
c/o Colombo Agencies Ltd.
No. 300-304, Galle Road
Colombo 3 Tel. (1) 574240, 573551-2
Fax: (1) 575394, 510711

SWEDEN – SUÈDE

CE Fritzes AB
S–106 47 Stockholm Tel. (08) 690.90.90
Fax: (08) 20.50.21

Subscription Agency/Agence d'abonnements :
Wennergren-Williams Info AB
P.O. Box 1305
171 25 Solna Tel. (08) 705.97.50
Fax: (08) 27.00.71

SWITZERLAND – SUISSE

Maditec S.A. (Books and Periodicals - Livres et périodiques)
Chemin des Palettes 4
Case postale 266
1020 Renens VD 1 Tel. (021) 635.08.65
Fax: (021) 635.07.80

Librairie Payot S.A.
4, place Pépinet
CP 3212
1002 Lausanne Tel. (021) 320.25.11
Fax: (021) 320.25.14

Librairie Unilivres
6, rue de Candolle
1205 Genève Tel. (022) 320.26.23
Fax: (022) 329.73.18

Subscription Agency/Agence d'abonnements :
Dynapresse Marketing S.A.
38, avenue Vibert
1227 Carouge Tel. (022) 308.07.89
Fax: (022) 308.07.99

See also – Voir aussi :
OECD Bonn Centre
August-Bebel-Allee 6
D-53175 Bonn (Germany) Tel. (0228) 959.120
Fax: (0228) 959.12.17

THAILAND – THAÏLANDE

Suksit Siam Co. Ltd.
113, 115 Fuang Nakhon Rd.
Opp. Wat Rajbopith
Bangkok 10200 Tel. (662) 225.9531/2
Fax: (662) 222.5188

TRINIDAD & TOBAGO

SSL Systematics Studies Limited
9 Watts Street
Curepe
Trinadad & Tobago, W.I. Tel. (1809) 645.3475
Fax: (1809) 662.5654

TUNISIA – TUNISIE

Grande Librairie Spécialisée
Fendri Ali
Avenue Haffouz Imm El-Intilaka
Bloc B 1 Sfax 3000 Tel. (216-4) 296 855
Fax: (216-4) 298.270

TURKEY – TURQUIE

Kültür Yayinlari Is-Türk Ltd. Sti.
Atatürk Bulvari No. 191/Kat 13
Kavaklidere/Ankara
Tel. (312) 428.11.40 Ext. 2458
Fax: (312) 417 24 90

Dolmabahce Cad. No. 29
Besiktas/Istanbul Tel. (212) 260 7188

UNITED KINGDOM – ROYAUME-UNI

HMSO
Gen. enquiries Tel. (0171) 873 0011
Postal orders only:
P.O. Box 276, London SW8 5DT
Personal Callers HMSO Bookshop
49 High Holborn, London WC1V 6HB
Fax: (0171) 873 8463
Branches at: Belfast, Birmingham, Bristol, Edinburgh, Manchester

UNITED STATES – ÉTATS-UNIS

OECD Washington Center
2001 L Street N.W., Suite 650
Washington, D.C. 20036-4922 Tel. (202) 785.6323
Fax: (202) 785.0350

Internet: washcont@oecd.org

Subscriptions to OECD periodicals may also be placed through main subscription agencies.

Les abonnements aux publications périodiques de l'OCDE peuvent être souscrits auprès des principales agences d'abonnement.

Orders and inquiries from countries where Distributors have not yet been appointed should be sent to: OECD Publications, 2, rue André-Pascal, 75775 Paris Cedex 16, France.

Les commandes provenant de pays où l'OCDE n'a pas encore désigné de distributeur peuvent être adressées aux Éditions de l'OCDE, 2, rue André-Pascal, 75775 Paris Cedex 16, France.

5-1996

OECD PUBLICATIONS, 2, rue André-Pascal, 75775 PARIS CEDEX 16
PRINTED IN FRANCE
(10 96 27 1) ISBN 92-64-15304-7 – No. 49013 1996
ISSN 0376-6438